THE
COMING
ECONOMIC
EARTHQUAKE

THE COMING ECONOMIC EARTHQUAKE

LARRY BURKETT

MOODY PRESS

CHICAGO

ISBN: 0-8024-1526-1

8 9 10 11 12 13 Printing/BC/Year 97 96 95 94 93 92

Printed in the United States of America

Contents

Introduction

Perhaps no force on earth creates more fear in the hearts of those who have experienced it than an earthquake. Those who have felt the very ground beneath their feet rolling and pitching will never forget the experience. It is the feeling of total and utter helplessness.

The forces moving the seemingly unmovable platform upon which we all live are beyond the wildest imagination of anything Hollywood can portray on the screen. They are the same forces that ripped the continents apart and set them adrift in the molten magma beneath the thin crust of earth.

I can recall descending into the steam caves of San Bernardino, California, and smelling the sulfur rising from the San Andreas fault. The heat seemed almost unbearable and was greatly amplified in my mind, knowing that this crack in the earth's surface could erupt violently at any time. The feeling I had was one of personal inconsequence. I was but an ant in comparison to the energy boiling up from the molten earth. I could hardly wait to ascend out of that closed-in space. And yet, I returned many times later just to experience the enormity of God's creation.

I have never experienced a major earthquake personally, although I have felt many minor quakes while visiting California. The few people I know who have felt the force of a major quake all expressed the same emotion: utter and complete terror—a feeling of being out of control.

Since this is not a book on seismology, or even geology, I will not elaborate any further at this point. But when the people at Moody asked me to write a book on the future of our economy, into the year 2000, I immediately thought of an analogy: an earthquake. I have not lived through an economic earthquake personally, but I have talked to several people who have. And I have read extensively about some of the better known economic earthquakes of the past. Without exception, those who lived through them expressed the same emotions as those who lived through geologic earthquakes: fear and helplessness.

I have often said that I am not a prophet of the Lord (in the sense that I have any ability to foretell the future) although we are all prophets in the sense that we should be able to "forthtell" the truth from God's Word. I say that as a prelude to this entire book.

This particular book is unlike anything I have ever written before. I'm going to step out on that proverbial limb and say what I believe is going to happen in our economy between now and the turn of the century. My timing may be off some, but I believe sincerely that my analysis is not. In many ways, it would be easier to leave this book unwritten. After all, why take the chance on being wrong? Several of my closest friends counseled me not to write it, "because if you're wrong," they said, "people will label you an alarmist, and if you're right, the others will say it's a fluke." I believe they are right on both counts, but I still have to say what I believe will happen. I trust that my insights are from the Lord and will help many of God's people to prepare now. If I'm wrong, anyone who follows the directions given in this book will be better off financially. If I'm right, they will be among the few to prosper in what may well be the greatest economic calamity of this millennium.

It is important to remember that earthquakes don't just happen. There are specific geological forces working that result in an eruption on the surface. Modern science knows very little about how to predict accurately *when* an earthquake will occur, but the scientists do know enough to predict accurately *where* one will occur. It doesn't take a geological wizard to see the San Andreas fault when flying over southern California. The ground is split open for hundreds of miles. Also, it doesn't take a Ph.D. in geology to predict that those living along that fault line are going to experience a first-class earthquake one day—up close and personal. Whether it will be this year, or in ten years, no one can predict accurately. But virtually no geologist of any report denies that pressures are building for a major movement.

The same can be said of our economy to a lesser degree. No economist of any report (outside government employment) denies that pressures are building in our economy that will erupt one day. Often they do disagree on the timing, the severity of the eruption, and the exact form it will take. And no one knows if it will be a gradual release of pressure or a Mount St. Helens blow-off. So it is up to you to decide if you want to wait and take your chances, or make some changes now.

I recall what the old curmudgeon Harry Truman said when the scientists warned him that Mount St. Helens might explode: "I've lived here nearly sixty years and it ain't blown yet." Mr. Truman now lies under forty feet of volcanic ash.

Just because the economy hasn't crashed yet doesn't mean it can't or won't. If enough of us believe it will and change our habits (and the government's), we might be able to avert it

One last thought before we begin: Personally I don't feel any anxiety about the future of our economy, nor am I the typical "doom and gloom" person. I do believe I am a realist and entirely pragmatic about the future. God will provide for those who follow His path and serve Him. But as Proverbs 16:9 says, "The mind of man plans his way, but the Lord directs his steps." I believe we are to use our minds in the service of our Lord.

I'll try to share as much as I know about the past, present, and future of our economy. You will have to decide for yourself if you want to do anything as a result.

People who live in earthquake regions often develop a fatalistic attitude toward the eventuality of a major eruption—until they actually experience one.

The same attitude prevails among those who have not experienced an economic earthquake. Those who lived through the Great Depression still remember and shudder at the thought. And those born after the Depression have a rude awakening in store.

1
Earthquake

The following narrative is a fictionalized account of what it is like to be really out of control.

As I was driving down the freeway, I began to notice the car swaying slightly. It felt as if a tire was low on air, so I slowed down, intending to pull into the freeway emergency lane. I didn't want to take a chance that a tire might go flat on the bridge ahead. As it turned out, that decision was probably all that saved my life.

As I slowed, I had a dizzy sensation, similar to vertigo. The freeway seemed to be undulating. But I knew that couldn't be, so I shook my head, trying to make some sense out of what I was feeling. Being a pilot, I knew that when anyone feels the sensation of vertigo, it is essential to focus on a fixed object to stabilize the equilibrium, so I concentrated on the concrete beams supporting the upper deck of the freeway.

But instead of clearing my vision, it seemed to blur even worse. The pillars, nearly two feet in diameter, seemed to vibrate in front of my eyes. I glanced down at the gauges on my dash and found I could not focus on them either. I began to panic as I feared I might be passing out.

It was several seconds before I realized what was wrong. The entire freeway seemed to be swaying as if some giant's hand was swinging it back and forth.

Earthquake! my mind screamed when I saw the concrete and asphalt begin to pitch upward as the whole structure swayed.

I had lived in the San Francisco area for more than twenty years and, as anyone who had lived in the "shaky" land for that long knows, earthquakes are a fact of life. Frequently, as I sat with my wife and children in our living room, we would feel a tremor ripple through our home. Usually it did little more than rattle the china; or a particularly strong tremor might move the furniture a couple of inches. Those little inconveniences are part of the price one pays for living on the Pacific rim.

Most geologists agree that the Pacific rim, from North America to the Philippine Islands, is some of the most geologically active habitat in the world. It is thought that the whole Pacific Ocean basin is slowly rotating. As it moves laterally to the continents, massive forces build up. When these forces release through rifts or faults, the results can be pretty startling, as anyone who lives along the rim can attest. The greatest threat to life and limb comes when one of the fault lines shear off and a major ground movement occurs.

That much I learned from my single course in geology at Southern Cal. It all seemed pretty academic back then. It doesn't anymore.

There had always been predictions of a big quake in the San Francisco area, and each time the prophets of doom had been wrong. In our office we even had "Richter pools" going whenever a major quake was predicted. The one closest to the actual rating of the quake won the pool. It was always the lucky people with a 4.5 (or less) reading on the Richter scale who won it.

We owned one of the newer homes in our area, one that had been designed to withstand quakes of up to a magnitude of 8, which is far beyond even the most pessimistic prophecies of doom. We felt safe knowing that even though everything around us might collapse in the "big one," we would survive.

The Nimitz freeway, which I traveled every day to and from the city, had been designed to California's stringent earthquake codes also. In fact, just a couple of months earlier, the state highway inspectors had given the Nimitz a clean "bill of health." "It will withstand the biggest quake this area will ever see," the director of transportation and safety (via the nightly news) assured those of us who commuted to the Bay area daily. In fact, the Japanese had sent some of their engineers over to study the structure. When they made comments that the freeway would not meet Japanese codes, the state engineers said it was a typical case of sour grapes. We discussed it at our office and decided it was the same old Japanese attitude: "If we didn't build it, it won't work." No one could look at that massive structure and believe anything could ever destroy it.

At first there was no sound. Then the structure began to moan as if it was alive and in heavy labor. Other sounds began to permeate the air: the creaking of unseen cables straining and snapping—like giant rubber bands breaking.

Most of the traffic was still moving, but as the overpasses swayed and bucked, panic-stricken drivers tried to stop their vehicles. Stopping on any freeway at any time of day is a lot like dodging a herd of stampeding buffalo; get in their way and you'll have hoof prints all over you.

> *I'm going to die, I told myself.*
> *I'm really going to die.*

Some drivers realized what was happening and tried to accelerate across the overpasses, attempting to outrun the calamity they sensed was inevitable. This quite effectively made stopping for any of the other drivers hazardous, if not impossible.

As I pulled off to the side, I was sure I was going to die. Already I could see cars being pitched from the upper decks plummeting downward. I could literally feel myself in their cars, hurtling toward certain death. I knew my turn would come as the section of structure I was on bucked and pitched out of sync with the upper tiers.

Still, there was no distinctive rumbling sound that I had always associated with an earthquake. But the sound from the concrete structure more than offset the lack of any familiar rumble. The creaking and groaning became a cacophony of sounds—more a feeling than a sound actually. Fear began to numb my senses to the point that I became an objective observer, rather than a participant.

I'm going to die, I told myself. *I'm really going to die. I wonder if Jan will remarry,* I thought pensively. *I hope so. I wouldn't want the kids to grow up without a father.* I quickly gave thanks that we had spent the extra money to earthquake-proof our home; then suddenly terror struck again. Sure! This is an earthquake-proof freeway, and look at what has happened to it!

Without warning, a deafening sound—like the clap of thunder—shattered the air, permeating the inside of my car. Ahead of me I saw the upper deck come crashing down. The cars beneath the massive concrete slabs simply disappeared. In the moment I had to watch, it seemed that they must have vanished, because the fallen deck appeared to settle flush with the pavement.

Clearly what the government and "experts" had touted as absolutely safe proved not to be.

I didn't have any time to ponder their fate as more of the upper structure thundered down around me. As the roof of the car was crushed in I thought, *Dear God, please protect my family.* Then everything went totally black.

It was a few seconds at most before I realized that I was still conscious. *Maybe I'm dead,* I thought. So I reached for where my leg should be and pinched—hard. The pain told me I probably wasn't dead. *But why not?* I wondered. I had seen what happened to the cars in front of me and knew instinctively that no car would support the weight of one of those sections of overpass.

I sat very still for what seemed like a long time, trying to sort out what had happened. I had driven that stretch of freeway for three years, but could remember almost nothing about its construction. Then I realized that when I pulled into the emergency lane I saw a concrete guard wall about the height of the upper part of my car window. It was apparently that wall that had stopped the fallen upper deck and saved my life. The roof was crushed in to the window level, but most of the compartment was intact. *But for how long?* I wondered.

Then I smelled gas fumes and terror struck. *Fire!* I thought as I envisioned the car enveloped in flames. "God, don't let me die like that," I cried out.

I reached for where the keys should be, trying to turn the ignition off. Debris from the concrete deck covered the inside of the car and apparently had stopped the engine as well. I turned the key off, praying that there would be no spark, and also praying that the gas from the other cars wouldn't ignite. Praise God, it didn't.

After what seemed like an hour or more, I heard faint sounds from somewhere outside. I yelled as loudly as I could, but couldn't tell if anyone heard me or not. It was certain I would not be able to get out of the car by myself; debris blocked the doors and windows. I had to force myself not to think about my family. *They will be okay,* I told myself over and over, trying to control my fear. *I have survived the worst part. Now I just have to hang on until help comes.*

Several minutes after the first sounds, I heard someone shouting, "Is anybody in there?"

"Yes," I yelled back as loudly as my hoarseness would allow.

"Hang on," he responded. "We've got help coming."

The sound of his voice brought hope; it was like being raised from the dead. *Someone knows I am alive. I'll be all right now,* I told myself. Then another form of terror set in and I thought, *What if they make a mistake and crush the car?* I didn't want to survive the freeway collapse just to die in a rescue attempt.

I experienced the same trepidation that many war-time veterans have when the fighting ends. They develop a paranoia about dying after having survived the battles.

Within an hour, the rescuers had reached my car and were clearing away some of the rubble from the driver's side window. One of them pulled me from the car and through an opening under the overhanging slab. He kept telling me, "Try to relax. You're going to be okay now." I knew I had made it.

The earthquake victim in this story was taken to the hospital for observation and then released a few hours later. He made his way back to his home through piles of littered debris from older buildings and homes that had crumbled during the earthquake that had measured 7.1 on the Richter scale. Unfortunately even some of supposed earthquake-proof buildings showed signs of structural faults, and many were later torn down. If the estimate of the "big" quake proved true at 8.0, it would be nine times more severe than this one!

There are signs throughout our economy of an impending earthquake.

He located his wife and children with friends whose home had suffered only minimal damage. Unfortunately his home, the home that had been built according to the latest earthquake standards, was totally destroyed, along with most of the other homes in their area.

Clearly what the government and "experts" had touted as absolutely safe proved not to be. The difference in whether or not someone's home was left standing depended upon where it was located, as much as how it was constructed. The experts had miscalculated the intensity of even what has to be considered a "moderate" earthquake when compared to the inevitable "big one" predicted for California.

It has long been my contention that the same analogy applies to the assessment of our government's rhetoric about our economic system being protected by a safety net of governmental regulations and controls. Personally, I don't subscribe to that theory. In my opinion, what we're being told is analogous to a building inspector finding a steam boiler grossly over pressurized and turning the dial on the gauge down until it reads in the green again. That may help the tenants to feel better temporarily, but it doesn't do anything for the basic problem.

There are signs throughout our economy of an impending earthquake. The tremors we have felt so far are just a little venting of steam, not an indication of how violent the blow-off can be. Unfortunately, each time some steam is vented and the economy doesn't collapse, the architects of the mess we now have say, "See there. I told you the system works."

Usually they also point to some "doom and gloom" person who ignorantly tried to pin a date on the blow-off just to sell a few more books. But just because their predictions didn't prove to be right, this in no way alters the basic facts: The generation in which we live has failed to learn from the past and is bound to repeat it.

Like the individuals in the San Francisco earthquake, if the experts are wrong, it's too late to do anything about it after the tremors start. The experts will come up with all kinds of excuses to show why they were wrong, but that's small consolation when the walls of your financial home crash down around you.

By the way, many of our earthquake victim's neighbors applied for and received government loans. Most rebuilt their homes on the very spots where they had been located previously. He rebuilt their home also, and then promptly sold it and moved to another state. You really can't do much about avoiding an earthquake, but move. So he did!

The Great Depression didn't just "happen." It was the culmination of more than two decades of economic abuse, during which time Americans used their new-found prosperity to speculate in the market.

With the zeal of the California gold rush, Americans risked all they had in an effort to strike it rich. They lost.

2
The Great Depression

The following is a narrated description of the events that took place the week of October 24-30, 1929. The narration is my creation; the events are historical fact.

Due to one of those quirks of fate, the president of the New York Stock Exchange, Edward Simmons, was in Hawaii on his honeymoon the last week of October 1929. His vice president, Richard Whitney, was in charge. Whitney had a long history as a habitual gambler and was deeply indebted to the New York banking interests. He was appointed as the president of the New York Stock Exchange in 1930, but later he went to prison for "insider trading."

Richard Whitney sat looking out the window of his twelfth-story office, trying to focus his mind on the current crisis but, no matter how hard he tried, he could not make any sense out of what was happening.

Can Bernard Baruch be right? he thought. *No, it's impossible. There is simply no way the market can collapse. We're the strongest economy in the world. We sell our products to every other nation on Earth. Just the label "made in America" stands for quality. Sure, the market has taken a hit, but the companies are still sound.*

He recalled the previous week when the whole of Wall Street had gone crazy. October 24 was a nightmare. As the buying frenzy hit the trading floor, Whitney saw something he would never forget as long as he lived, and he prayed to God he would never see again: nearly twelve million shares of common stocks traded in a single afternoon. No sooner had one level of trading been established than another ten thousand shares were offered. The men who had manipulated the sell-off were like sharks waiting for their victims to bleed to death. They refused to buy until the prices dropped to their predetermined level. Even AT&T, GE, and GM plummeted to dangerous lows as panic-stricken investors, fearing a market collapse, sold off shares.

> *Although few men realized it*
> *at the time, the finances*
> *of America were in shambles,*
> *and the thin veneer of prosperity*
> *covered a festering wound.*

Whitney would have closed the exchange, but he feared the resulting reaction would be even worse. Besides, he knew President Hoover would be very irritated if he intervened in the market. The president believed in a free market, where the buyers and sellers established the rules.

But I know the bankers are manipulating this market for their own benefit, Whitney thought grimly. *They make more on their stock portfolios than they do on loans these days. They pump up a stock and then dump it on the unsuspecting little guys. The newspapers grovel at their feet and hype their stocks so that the whole country is in the market now.*

It's like Baruch said at lunch last week: "When the shoeshine boy starts giving tips on hot stocks to buy, it's time to get out of the market."

I really fear what could happen if we don't get some control over these swings in prices, Whitney thought as he went back over the day's trading. *We've lost almost $100 million in equity in the last week. Well, tomorrow is Friday. If we can weather this storm, maybe common sense will prevail by Monday,* he told himself without any real conviction.

What Whitney didn't know was that since the big traders had sold out at top price on the 24th, they intended to drive the prices down even further by calling the loans of some of the margin traders who were stretched thin. If the bankers could force them to sell in the down market, prices would plummet. Then they would re-buy their original stocks and pocket the difference.

"A smart man makes his money with money," J. P. Morgan was often heard to say, and, "God wouldn't have made sheep if he didn't expect them to be sheared."

Although few men realized it at the time, the finances of America were in shambles, and the thin veneer of prosperity covered a festering wound. The industrialists and bankers had succeeded in getting laws passed by the federal government that profited them greatly while undermining the economy as a whole.

The country was on a roll, and no one really thought it would come to an end.

America was producing more than the country could consume internally. Through the use of high-interest loans, borrowers were transferring their wealth to the industrialists and bankers on a scale never witnessed before. The industrialists, with their political power, had been instrumental in getting Congress to pass restrictive trade laws limiting imports. As they lost more of their foreign markets due to retaliatory restrictions, inventories were backing up. Unemployment was becoming a chronic problem for the "underclass"; production was slowing down; and loans were becoming commonplace.

The bankers were making huge "paper" profits through loans that often carried interest rates of 20 percent or more. The competition for loans became so intense that bankers eased loan qualifications to attract more borrowers.

The average American watched the money merchants getting wealthy in the stock market and flocked to the market to "strike it rich." Lacking the capital to invest, they financed a large portion of their speculation with the bankers. With virtually no controls on market trading, any speculator could hold blocks of stocks with as little as 10 percent down. If that stock was then used as collateral for more loans, the ratio could easily be fifty-to-one.

It was a win-win situation for the lenders. They loaned the money for small investors to buy the very stocks they themselves were forcing up through manipulation. Then, when the prices fell, the small speculators would borrow more to cover their losses. It was one of the most massive transfers of wealth in the history of civilization. It was the era of "paper" prosperity—the Roaring Twenties, when America could do no wrong. The country was on a roll, and no one really thought it would come to an end.

There were those voices of "doom and gloom" who shook their fingers and clicked their tongues, but their ominous predictions of calamity had not come true—yet.

On Monday, October 28, the New York Stock Exchange opened normally. Richard Whitney arrived at his Wall Street office at 7:00 A.M., as was his custom. Inwardly he was full of apprehension, though he tried his best not to show it. He had spent the weekend calling in every favor he had accumulated over the past ten years. His greatest fear was a run on the market by nervous investors who had the entire weekend to discuss the previous week's losses with their barroom buddies. He knew many, if not most, were heavily leveraged and could scarcely afford any further losses.

Sunday evening he had called Charles Mitchell of the National City Bank. "Charles, I need your help," he said as he unconsciously fingered the phone wire.

"What is it, Richard?" the banker asked, showing his irritation at being interrupted on the weekend. The all-day session on Saturday with his directors had been fatiguing enough. The bank's questionable debt list was growing at an alarming rate. *That's justice*, he thought. *They pressure me to make loans, then wonder why we have a collection problem.*

"I'm concerned that we may have a run tomorrow," Whitney said. "I want your guarantee that you and the others will support the market if necessary."

"Richard, there's not going to be any run on the market. Not tomorrow. Not ever. The country is doing just fine, and the market hasn't nearly reached its peak. We just pulled a little capital out. It will recover this week."

"I hope you're right." Whitney replied, with concern evident in his voice. "But I still want your word that you'll support the market if necessary. I don't want you pulling the plug on credit and sinking the whole ship."

"I guarantee that we'll support you, Richard. But I'm telling you, you're worrying too much. The country is sound, business is good, and we've got a president who understands how to keep the government off our backs. Now take it easy."

The traders were all assembled in the trading room of the exchange by eight o'clock that Monday morning. Each had a preset agenda for the trading he would do that day. Each would also try to hide his agenda until the others made a move. Promptly at nine o'clock, the bell rang and trading got underway. Richard Whitney watched from his glassed-in office to see what direction the market would follow. He almost called Mitchell again, but decided against it. *No sense in panicking*, he told himself.

The pace on the floor was frenzied as buyers and sellers jockeyed for position. The buyers were looking for bargains. The sellers were waiting in hopes that demand would drive the prices up. Shares began trading rapidly as cash-strapped smaller investors offered to sell some of their stocks.

By ten o'clock there was no definitive trend; the buyers and sellers were about even, with only a slight downward drift.

Whitney slumped back in his leather chair in relief. "That's fine," he said to the board auditor. "We can handle a drift downward. *We dodged the bullet this time,* he said mentally.

By the close of trading at four o'clock, the averages had dropped by twenty points. *Not an abnormal trading loss for the market on any given down day,* Whitney thought as he stuffed the latest trading reports into his briefcase and headed out the door. Normally he would have reviewed the reports before leaving, but he was mentally exhausted. The tension had kept him uptight for nearly a week now, and somehow he sensed it wasn't entirely over yet.

Millions of Americans lost their life savings, and thousands of millionaires became more statistics in the growing ranks of the unemployed.

On Tuesday, October 29, the market opened just as it had for two decades. No one had any particular sense of apprehension or anxiety. Most of the major traders assumed that Monday had been the real test of the market's resiliency; and although it had not set any growth records, at least there were no major cracks either.

When the Exchange opened for business, the trading volume quickly reached the level of the previous day, except that virtually all the trades were sell orders. The market plunged as more sellers flooded the floor. Once the plunge started, it was like Whitney's worst nightmare. The radio carried the bad news to the American people and more sell orders flooded in from panic-stricken investors, fearful of losing their savings. It was like a gigantic economic snowball—as more sellers panicked, fewer buyers would step forward.

As the frenzied trading continued, even the veteran traders knew this was not just another down day on the market. It was a true sell-off of all stocks. Even the traditional "blue chippers" were being dumped.

By the ending bell, AT&T was down 100 points, General Motors down 150 points, General Electric down 90 points. More than 16 million shares were traded at a loss of $10 billion—twice the amount of currency in the entire country at that time. Whitney knew that without major support from the big banks, the market would continue the tumble when the bell sounded the next morning. Even with their support, he wasn't at all sure the selling could be halted.

The evening newspapers all carried the headline: "Wall Street Crashes." By the next morning, virtually every small investor in the country had issued a sell order, hoping to salvage something of their equity.

Panic ruled the market from that fateful Tuesday on. There were small rallies where determined investors attempted to support their portfolio of stocks. But those who did, quickly found themselves among the destitute. Millions of Americans lost their life savings, and thousands of millionaires became just more statistics in the growing ranks of the unemployed.

People who had grown up in the American enterprise system and thought it could not be defeated were swallowed up as banks, businesses, farms, and homes all fell victim to what would be called "The Great Depression."

One story in a New York newspaper told of a ship full of wealthy entrepreneurs who, on the return portion of their vacations, sailed from England the last week of October. The ship had been equipped with the latest telegraph equipment so the men could keep abreast of their stocks during the voyage. By the 30th of October, as the market plummeted, they could no longer place sell orders and expect them to be executed, and by the time they arrived in New York on the 4th of November, they owned little more than what they had with them on the ship.

One of the most publicized aspects of the Wall Street collapse was the specter of suicides by once-prominent traders. Men who had lost their entire fortunes often committed suicide by jumping from their offices high above Wall Street. But as alarming as this was, it paled when compared to the misery the average American worker and his family suffered over the succeeding decade.

By the end of the year, the Stock Market had lost the unbelievable sum of $40 billion in equity, taking with it hundreds of banks and millions of jobs. By 1932, the depth of the Depression, more than five thousand banks had closed their doors; leaving millions of depositors with nothing to show for their thrift. The national income plummeted from over $80 billion in 1929 to less than $40 billion by 1932. The promise of prosperity built on debt had tempted normally conservative Americans to risk all they owned. They lost.

In 1928 there was no venture too harebrained for a banker to fund, if the interest rate was high enough. By 1930 there was no legitimate venture, no matter what its merit, that could find an interested banker. Speculators, such as Bernard Baruch, who had withdrawn their assets from the market before the collapse, used their hard currency to buy land, businesses, and the lifetime efforts of others for a fraction of their actual worth. Even the "big banks" were on the ropes. The men who had manipulated the market for their own benefit found the pond rapidly drying up.

> *What we accept as normal today,
> any generation prior to the
> Great Depression would have
> seen as unconstitutional.*

Hypocritically, most of those who had once insisted that the government should stay out of the regulating business now cried for government aid. Their cries fell on deaf ears in the White House. Herbert Hoover had been elected because of his laissez faire policy, and he was not about to renege on what he believed. He did attempt a few government programs to help the unemployed and homeless, but most were aimed at easing poverty, not stimulating business. His philosophy was, "If business created the mess, business should repair it."

Most economists since the Depression have faulted Hoover for his nonintervention. Perhaps a good case can be made for the administration's lack of control prior to the Depression, but there had been several previous depressions in America from which the nation recovered without direct government intervention, so the president felt justified in following historical precedent.

Without a government bailout, using taxpayers' money, the Depression of 1837 had lasted but four years; the Depression of 1893, four years; and the panics (recessions) of 1904, 1907, and 1921 lasted less than two years each.

But with millions of voters out of work, and the big banks in trouble, Hoover could garner no support for his reelection. The nation was ready for a change: a "New Deal," as the Democratic party promised.

Their spokesman for this New Deal was an articulate aristocrat with a household family name: Roosevelt. Franklin Roosevelt was born to wealth, raised in wealth, and educated in wealth at Harvard, where he was exposed to the philosophies of Dr. John Maynard Keynes of England. Keynes, an avowed socialist, had long advocated the use of government control over banking and business to ensure prosperity for all. The philosophy was not new. Karl Marx had advocated essentially the same doctrine, only to a more radical group—the poor.

> *The Depression set the stage for the federal government to dominate American business, banking, commerce, and the economy as a whole.*

Keynes' economic theory had yet to be tested in a sizeable system. But, with America in depression, it was about to be implemented wholeheartedly. That now suited the bankers and industrialists perfectly because they desperately needed an infusion of capital to hold on to what they had siphoned out of the general public. The New Deal would forevermore change the average American's view of the role of their central government.

I have presented this brief overview of the Depression of 1929 because so few Americans are aware of how it began—or ended. Most of those who lived through the Depression were scarred for life. Most unemployed voters viewed Franklin Roosevelt as truly their economic "savior." And in fairness, President Roosevelt did what he believed was the right thing to do, in spite of the Supreme Court's view to the contrary. But so profoundly is the New Deal philosophy now ingrained in American politics that, in order to understand the coming "economic earthquake," it is critical to understand how our government functions monetarily.

What we accept as normal today, any generation prior to the Great Depression would have seen as unconstitutional. According to the Constitution, the central (federal) government is to have no powers except those specifically granted it by the Constitution. All other rights and powers not specifically granted the individual states are preserved for their citizens. That includes the right to succeed or fail according to one's own abilities, unrestrained by the government. So fearful were the founders of this country of a strong central government that they went to great lengths to ensure that its powers were severely limited. Basically, the central government could settle arguments between the states, organize an army to defend the nation's common cause, regulate interstate commerce, and negotiate foreign treaties. The federal government was allowed to raise its operating capital by charging an interstate tariff on goods only—period!

The Depression set the stage for the federal government to dominate American business, banking, commerce, and the economy as a whole. Franklin Roosevelt raised the status of the federal government to that of the "great provider." Whether or not you agree or disagree with the New Deal, no one can deny it changed American politics and the economy forever.

In my opinion, it also set the stage for an eventual economic disaster unparalleled in American history. As you will see, the events that led us to this point are not unique. Others have traveled this economic road before us. The major difference between us and them is our size and influence. It is my considered opinion that our nation has prospered because of a unique commitment to God's divine authority. We are now traveling a path that is almost totally contrary to that original commitment. It would be wise to note God's instruction to the Jews:

> Now it shall be, if you will diligently obey the Lord your God, being careful to do all His commandments which I command you today, the Lord your God will set you high above all the nations of the earth. And all these blessings shall come upon you and overtake you, if you will obey the Lord your God. Blessed shall you be in the city, and blessed shall you be in the country. . . . The Lord will open for you His good storehouse, the heavens, to give rain to your land in its season and to bless all the work of your hand; and you shall lend to many nations, but you shall not borrow. And the Lord shall make you the head and not the tail, and you only shall be above, and you shall not be underneath, if you will listen to the commandments of the Lord your God, which I charge you today, to observe them carefully, and do not turn aside from any of the words which I command you today, to the right or to the left, to go after other gods to serve them (Deuteronomy 28:1-3, 12-14).

Now observe His warning to them:

> But it shall come about, if you will not obey the Lord your God, to observe to do all His commandments and His statutes with which I charge you today, that all these curses shall come upon you and overtake you. . . . The alien who is among you shall rise above you higher and higher, but you shall go down lower and lower. He shall lend to you but you shall not lend to him; he shall be the head, and you shall be the tail. So all these curses shall come on you and pursue you and overtake you until you are destroyed, because you would not obey the Lord your God by keeping His commandments and His statutes which He commanded you (Deuteronomy 28:15, 43-45).

With Americans mired in the bog of the deepest depression in history, the "New Deal" administration promised them strong leadership and a government handout.

The long-term effects of the New Deal have outlasted the short-term benefits to the thirties generation. Nearly 80 percent of all Americans now draw some form of government subsidy.

3
The New Deal

I have always been fascinated by history. I sometimes think I was born into the wrong century because there is little demand for historians in our generation. Today it seems that people are seeking prophets more than historians. And yet, the future becomes much clearer in the light of history. There are two old cliches that I appreciate very much: "Those who fail to learn from the past are doomed to repeat it." and "The more things change, the more they stay the same."

We think we generate new ideas, but in reality we only keep modifying some old ideas that previous generations thought they created. Such an idea was the New Deal.

Franklin Roosevelt was elected at the depth of the Depression, in 1932, based on a catchy slogan his party had adopted from the Republicans: "a chicken in every pot." Only this time, it would be a *government* chicken in every pot. The promise was to restore the American economy, no matter what the cost. It was a clear trade-off between the short-term needs of families in a depression and freedom from government controls. According to the interpretation of the Constitution at that time, there was simply no way that the federal government could give taxpayers' money to private individuals, no matter how justified it seemed. In order to get its agenda passed, the Roosevelt administration had to literally reinterpret the Constitution. The founding fathers had created a remarkable system of checks and balances that ensured that no short-term crisis could undermine the long-term rights of American citizens, even if the citizens wanted to do so, which clearly the thirties generation did.

The New Deal designers had a four-item agenda they wanted to implement:

1. Initiate direct transfers of payments (dubbed "entitlements") to Americans who needed help

2. Establish the federal government as an overseer and regulator of American business—particularly banking

3. Establish a strong central banking system to regulate all monetary policy

4. Establish a national depositors' insurance program.

Grover Cleveland best stated
the prevailing policy. . .
"It is the responsibility of the
citizens to support their government.
It is not the responsibility of the
government to support its citizens."

Taken individually, each of these ideas were radical enough but, collectively, they represented the most sweeping changes in America since the framing of the Constitution. Perhaps the president could have convinced the American people to amend the Constitution to allow these adaptations, but time did not permit the process. So he attempted to implement them through legislation—virtually all of which the Supreme Court ruled unconstitutional. This set off a six-year battle between the president and the court, which eventually ended with the replacement of the dissenting majority of the court by 1939.

In the meantime, the agenda went forward through the well-established political process known as "stonewalling." This is where Congress creates a law, which the president signs and implements, such as relief payments to farmers for farm price supports. The Supreme Court vetoes the law as unconstitutional, but since the funds have already been distributed, they cannot be recovered. Congress then passes another very similar law, which the president signs and implements. The new law is later vetoed by the court again. And so the process goes on year after year, until enough of the court is replaced that presidential policy becomes constitutionally acceptable. With no limit to the number of consecutive terms a president could serve, it was simply a matter of whether Roosevelt would outlive the older court members. He did.

> *Americans were dependent on the redistribution of taxpayers' funds by the federal government for the first time in our short democracy.*

I would like to review briefly the agenda (policies) of the New Deal administration, because understanding these four policies is essential to understanding the future of our economy.

POLICY NUMBER 1:
ENTITLEMENTS

Perhaps President Grover Cleveland best stated the prevailing policy concerning transfer payments from the federal government to private citizens when he made his historic stand against helping a deserving orphanage in New York City during a severe economic crisis: "I will not be a party to stealing money from one group of citizens to give to another group of citizens; no matter what the need or apparent justification. Once the coffers of the federal government are open to the public, there will be no shutting them again." He went on to conclude, "It is the responsibility of the citizens to support their government. It is not the responsibility of the government to support its citizens."

In Cleveland's generation, another politician wrote, "A democracy is not a form of government to survive. For it will only succeed until its citizens discover they can vote themselves money from the treasury, then they will bankrupt it." That politician was Karl Marx.

Under the New Deal, a variety of direct entitlement programs were started, including the Civilian Conservation Corps (CCC), in which citizens were employed by the federal government to work on public projects. These projects ranged all the way from one group digging holes that another group filled in to constructing hydroelectric dams.

In addition, the farm support program paid farmers to take certain crops out of production to raise the prices. Often farmers were paid to grow crops and then were required to plow them under in order to receive their subsidies.

Social Security was designed to ensure that all Americans had some retirement, disability, and survivors' death benefits.

By 1938 the federal government had transferred nearly $60 billion in revenues to the farmers, the unemployed, the retired, the sick, and sometimes lazy Americans. The first step of the New Deal was entrenched and irrevocable. Americans were dependent on the redistribution of taxpayers' funds by the federal government for the first time in our short democracy.

To be fair, I need to point out that some of the programs had great merit. Child labor was abolished, natural resources (such as the Colorado River and the Tennessee Valley) were developed, and a variety of other good programs were started. But many of these were already in progress before the New Deal arrived. Child labor was rapidly vanishing in the industrialized north and west simply because machines could do the jobs faster and cheaper. Several states already had efficient resource development projects underway when the Depression struck. They lacked the resources to continue the projects but would have done so after the Depression ended.

POLICY NUMBER 2:
GOVERNMENT REGULATIONS

For most Americans alive today, the idea that the federal government can force car companies to increase their gas mileage or install safety belts is totally acceptable. We also accept the policy that the Occupational Safety and Health Administration (OSHA) should inspect a business to ensure that it complies with federal standards for workers' safety. We accept the mandate of the Environmental Protection Agency (EPA) to require all businesses to meet federal environment standards. And the list goes on.

Certainly some of these federal agencies do a good job and provide a needed service, but the issue is really a broader one: Is this a legitimate role of our government? Prior to the New Deal, most Americans would have said emphatically, "No!"

Deciding where to draw that line is a difficult task. Few historians would disagree that the federal government did too little in the way of regulating the banks and stock market prior to the collapse in '29. But once that pendulum swings, it usually goes to the opposite extreme, as apparently it now has.

It is an interesting parallel that many of the same policies were being instituted in Germany at this time.

Roosevelt shut down all the banks under the laws of the New Deal and reopened them with strict federal controls, including a strong central bank and federally insured deposits. From this base, the government branched out to touch virtually every business in America. Using cheap federal credit, the New Deal established controls over how many tractors were built, and at what price. Homes financed with federal monies had to be built according to the Federal Housing Authority's codes. Farmers who wouldn't join the land bank program found their credit cut off. Even states that didn't adopt federal standards for schools, roads, sewage, etc. were in jeopardy of having their supplemental federal funds cut off. Money became an effective social weapon to place the federal government at the top of all planning.

It is an interesting parallel that many of the same policies were being instituted in Germany at this time. The Nazis enforced their rule through force. The New Deal strategists enforced theirs through financial intimidation. The term "fascist," which is normally applied to Nazi Germany, is equally applicable to the American economy. The term simply means "privately owned but centrally controlled."

POLICY NUMBER 3:
A CENTRAL BANK

President Woodrow Wilson had been successful in getting the Federal Reserve Banking Act passed into law; but in reality, it was little more than a paper system. The strong independent banks called the shots, and the Federal Reserve followed obediently. The New Deal changed all that. With virtually all the banks on the brink of collapse, President Roosevelt succeeded in establishing the Federal Reserve Board as the authority in banking. Independent banks were not forced to join the Federal Reserve System. But those that did not found they could not transact business through any member bank. Once the member banks' deposits were insured through the Federal Depositors Insurance Corporation (FDIC), the death of the nonaligned banks was just a matter of time.

Unfortunately, the same system that makes it possible for banks to multiply their deposits into loans also makes them vulnerable to defaults by borrowers.

With the Federal Reserve Banking system in place, the administration had a potent weapon to fight swings in the economy. The central bank could inflate the currency (the New Deal also dropped the gold standard and made the ownership of gold illegal); it could reallocate funds to distressed areas through loans; and it could create money out of thin air through the use of "fractional banking."

Fractional banking is so fundamental to our later discussion of the coming economic earthquake, I would like to digress for a moment and give a brief overview of the fractional banking system.

The central bank (Federal Reserve) establishes a minimum reserve requirement for all member banks. This policy is meant to maintain a reserve in the central bank that can be used to help members when necessary. The money is loaned to members, who then can lend it to distressed citizens; at least that was the rationale behind it. Two factors become important in such a reserve system: the reserve requirement and the discount rate (the interest paid to the Reserve for members to borrow money). Requiring member banks to set aside reserves at no interest and then borrow from the reserves at interest would seem to be a difficult policy to sell, unless the system offered them something in return. Let's look at an example of how the Federal Reserve and "fractional banking" aids its members.

In our example, let's assume that the Fed (Federal Reserve) required member banks to deposit 10 percent of all their deposits with the central bank. Now let's assume that a member bank accepts a customer's deposit of $1,000. You would logically assume it would send 10 percent ($100) to the Fed. Right? Wrong. Instead, it sends the entire $1,000, representing assumed deposits of $10,000. The bank then lends an imaginary $9,000 to its customers.

Where did they get this money to lend? That's the function of the centralized system of "cooperating" banks. They don't actually have the money. Each member bank agrees to accept the "paper" of the other banks. So the loan is honored the same as cash when deposited. It works even better if the borrower deposits the "loan money" in the issuing bank. Each deposit becomes collateral for additional loans and member banks can lend as much as *700 percent* of actual cash deposits.

Unfortunately, the same system that makes it possible for banks to multiply their deposits into loans also makes them vulnerable to defaults by borrowers. With scant reserves, the banks must depend even more heavily on the central bank, further securing the system. Look around and see how many nonmember banks survive today.

POLICY NUMBER 4:
NATIONAL DEPOSITORS' INSURANCE

As mentioned before, the benefits of a guaranteed depositors' insurance plan attracted many banks into the Federal Reserve System. It serves one more function that has a long-term detrimental effect on the whole economy. Depositors are less concerned about the lending policies of their banks.

Perhaps the leading opposition economist of the Roosevelt era was Dr. Ludwig Von Mises. Dr. Von Mises, having lived through the Depression in Germany after World War I, had seen the devastating effects of uncontrolled government "management" of the monetary system.

Von Mises states in his book, *Money, Method, and the Market System*: "Banks which promise (depositors) no more than they can fulfill without extraordinary assistance from the central bank never jeopardize the stability of the country's currency. . . . If the central banks did not believe it was their duty to cover up the consequences of the deposit banks' errors in lending, they could not jeopardize the assets of the prudent bankers."

There are many noted economists
who believe the New Deal dealt
the American economy a death blow
that has taken nearly sixty years
to surface fully.

Essentially, Von Mises said, and later proved, if the abuses get widespread enough, even the central bank (or the FDIC) cannot cover the losses. Ultimately the government will either inflate the currency to pay the bills or it will tax its citizens to do so. Since the government's ability to tax is limited to what the taxpayers will accept, it becomes politically more expedient to inflate the currency through debt accumulation.

Certainly what we have seen in the demise of the Savings and Loans associations testifies to this analysis. What we have not yet seen is the effect of billions (or trillions) of dollars of government debt coming due. The certainty is that no debt can be accumulated indefinitely. The compound interest curve eventually makes even the payment of interest impossible.

There are many noted economists who believe the New Deal dealt the American economy a death blow that has taken nearly sixty years to surface fully. We live in a highly regulated economy, run by people whose only claim to success is getting elected to a government office. No one can deny that the federal entitlements program is out of control. It consumes nearly 70 percent of all government spending now. Almost 80 percent of all Americans draw some form of direct or indirect government subsidy.

The central banking system now determines interest rates for virtually every bank in the country. A change in the reserve requirement or discount policy will affect the lives of every American, regardless of their economic status.

Government regulation has become so pervasive that between the EEOC, OSHA, EPA, IRS, and so on, no business escapes government interference. More and more businesses are being relocated to less controlled countries with the resultant loss of millions of jobs in America. Often entire industries live or die according to the whims and wishes of officials who are not subject to any election, veto, or control by the citizens who pay their salaries.

The national bank insurance plan has been so abused that now taxpayers are being "asked" to cough up nearly *three thousand dollars* each to pay for the S&L losses. This is the logical consequence of allowing a system to operate devoid of any local controls. Because their funds were "insured," depositors simply didn't know or care that their local S&L was making stupid loans, as well as helping many managers live like kings.

The seeds sown in the New Deal administration are still growing in our economy today. Once the process is started, it is very difficult to correct!

For those who lived through a decade of depression, there was an indelible imprint that can never be erased. For every available job, there were a hundred applicants.

Tens of thousands of homeless people drifted across the country searching for nothing more than enough food to sustain life for one more day.

No one had believed the prosperity of the twenties could end so quickly. A few people prospered, but millions lived in despair.

4
Life in a Depression

The previous chapter gave a brief description of what the start of the Great Depression was like from inside the stock market. But that was only the beginning of a decade of economic hard times. It was the average American family who felt the real brunt of an economy that was plunged into the longest depression in U.S. history.

At one point, nearly 40 percent of all available workers were unemployed, causing a trauma so great it can only be grasped by those who lived it. America was a country without hope, at least economically. The middle class virtually disappeared. There were the rich who prospered through and even because of the depression, and there were the others who had lost everything.

To understand the impact of the Great Depression, we must return to the decade leading up to the collapse. This era was called the Roaring Twenties, appropriately named because society was roaring—both economically and socially.

Almost 70 percent of all Americans lived in rural communities that supported the farming industry. Agriculture was the primary business of America. For the most part, farmers were hard-working, family-oriented people whose social lives revolved around their churches. Elections were held in the church, politicians spoke to constituents there, even public schools met in church buildings. The vast majority of Americans believed in God, attended church regularly, and considered themselves to be moral, ethical people.

The successful conclusion of World War I established America as the world leader in virtually every category.

The same could not be said about all Americans though—especially those in the entertainment, political, or money-lending business. Often their lives revolved around gaudy shows, gross immorality, gangsters, and crooked politicians.

The successful conclusion of World War I established America as the world leader in virtually every category: economics, military, entertainment, and social "graces." The Vanderbilts, Carnegies, Morgans, and Kennedys became the socially elite, replacing the European gentry.

When Americans turned their energies toward producing goods, they simply out-produced the entire world. It was a time of unprecedented economic prosperity, led by a mechanized revolution in industry and agriculture. For the first time in the history of mankind, less than one-half of the working force could provide enough food for the majority and still have plenty left to export for sale. By the end of the twenties, farm efficiency had improved so greatly that only 20 percent of the working force was needed on the farms; 80 percent was freed to work in other areas of production.

In addition to being relieved from heavy labor and long hours on the farm, Americans were confronted with a plethora of new products. Automobiles were within the reach of average wage earners; homes were available on long-term financing (up to seven years); refrigerators, washing machines, radios, gas stoves, and the like were all flooding onto the market.

Credit cards were not yet invented, but consumer credit was readily available from willing merchants who knew that their friends and neighbors would pay their bills.

It was in this time of prosperity that the average savings rate of Americans declined from 12 percent of their incomes to less than 4 percent. The reason was twofold: There were many new products they wanted and no real need for pessimism about the future. The Republicans had originally coined the term "a chicken in every pot" to describe the prosperity that Americans were enjoying under their leadership.

The attitudes of the average American can be understood best by looking into the lives of a family who lived through this period of prosperity and the depression that followed.

The following story is based on past conversations with a personal friend. The narration is mine; the descriptions are his.

I had been working at the Ford Motor Company for nearly four years by 1929. Times were good in Detroit, and buyers flocked to the car showrooms every year as soon as the new models came out.

By 1929 old Henry (Ford) agreed that Ford buyers could have a choice of colors and style. Until 1925 Ford buyers could have any color they wanted, as long as it was black! But with Chevrolets outselling Fords, Mr. Ford had given in to his designers, who wanted to make several models and colors available. The change perked up the "A model" sales.

After renting for the first seven years of our marriage, Mary and I bought our first home. We had to finance nearly three thousand dollars, even after her father gave us a thousand dollars for the downpayment. I figured it would be worth it in the long run, though. The payments were nearly fifty dollars a month, which scared us both a little, but I had a good job and the money was budgeted. With car sales being so good, the plant was running double shifts, plus overtime. *After all*, I reasoned, *I work for one of the biggest companies in America, and prospects have never been better; why not buy a home?*

I kept reading about all the money being made in the stock market, and some of the other men on my shift had even borrowed money to invest. One of the guys, Bobby Thomas, bragged how he had made $600 in one month. Maybe he did, but he was known to exaggerate—a lot. Mary and I talked about investing, but she argued that we needed things for the house more than we needed stocks. I knew she was probably right, but it sure looked like an easier way to make money than working on an assembly line.

The last week in October 1929, I heard several of the men talking about how the stock market had dropped suddenly, and a lot of people feared it would drop some more. I had read about it in the papers—they called it the biggest drop in the history of the stock market—but I didn't think much about it then. After all, we didn't have any stocks, and Mr. Ford was so rich it surely couldn't affect him very much. The thing that did bother me was how much attention the stock market drop was getting around the plant. They made it sound like the end of the world might happen any day. When Mary seemed worried, I said, "Honey, even if people lose money in the stock market, I don't see what difference it makes. After all, they didn't have the money before the stocks went up, did they?"

"No, I guess you're right," she told me. But it still worried her. And deep inside, it worried me some too. I just didn't like things happening that I had no control over.

I was working first shift on Tuesday, when someone came racing into the plant yelling that the market had collapsed. In a few minutes the whole plant was buzzing about it. I wondered, *Why is everyone so upset because stock prices dropped?* So I asked Bobby Thomas. He said, "It means a lot of people are going to get wiped out." With that, he took his work apron off and left the plant.

Later I learned that he had borrowed a lot of money from his wife's parents, who were farmers, and he had lost it all. I never saw him again, because they packed up and moved to escape their creditors.

I left work that evening with a sense of dread like I had never felt before. From all the conversations I overheard, it was obvious that the stock market crash was going to affect more than just some stock investors. The evening papers made it sound like America had just lost a war. I began to realize that the comfort level I had felt just a week earlier was rapidly disappearing. Mary was pregnant with our third child and I didn't want to lose my job—not when we had just bought a home.

When I got home Mary was listening to the radio. "What does it mean?" she asked as soon as I walked in the door.

"I don't know," I told her. I was so mentally exhausted I just dropped into one of our well-worn chairs. I had stopped on the way home to pick up the "Extra" edition of the paper, which told all about the stock market crash. It read like the world was collapsing, right along with the stock market.

"Betty Alterman from my Sunday School class called and said she heard the banks are in trouble," Mary told me fretfully.

"I don't see how that's possible," I assured her. But the frown I must have been wearing didn't hide my inner feelings.

I hadn't even thought about the banks! I tried to visualize the large brick bank building and the massive safe that was protecting our money. *How could a bank fail just because of the stock market?* I asked myself. I didn't know the answer, but I wanted to avoid upsetting Mary, so I tried to hide what I was feeling.

"Do you think we should draw out our savings?" Mary asked me. I noticed her soft brown eyes were moist. "It's only sixty dollars, but it's all we have. I was going to use some of it to have the furniture recovered."

It had only been two weeks since the crash, and I was out of a job, had no money, and had a wife and two kids to feed.

"There's just no way a big bank like First National could fold just because of a stock market problem," I told her confidently. "We're at least 650 miles from New York City, so how could it effect our bank here in Detroit?"

Little did I know at that time how wrong I was. Not only did the market crash affect our bank, it affected every bank in Detroit. As the situation worsened, reports of bank failures in New York panicked depositors all over the country. Within a few days lines formed outside every bank, waiting for them to open so people could get their money out.

President Hoover appealed to the public not to panic, and he assured Americans that the country was still "as sound as a dollar." But the lines still formed every day.

Finally I told Mary we should get our money out too. But I had waited a day too long, because the day Mary went to stand in line, the bank never opened its doors. A bank employee came out and told everyone the bank had run out of money and wouldn't be opening again.

"What's going to happen?" Mary asked as we lay in bed that evening, unable to sleep. "Every day things seem to get worse instead of better. Will you lose your job?"

"I don't know, honey," I answered as I tried to sort out what had happened in the last week. "Ford is a big company. I don't think it could be in trouble." But even as I tried to comfort Mary, I knew the awful truth: the whole country is in trouble.

The newspapers were full of reports of companies failing. There were even reports of rich people who had lost everything jumping out of windows.

The next Monday, when I went to work, our shift was told to wait before clocking in; the shift supervisor wanted to talk to us.

I had that feeling of dread again. I knew what he was going to say. We all did. We just hated to admit that it could happen to us. Two weeks ago we were working overtime to produce cars because the demand was so great, but in the last week orders had dropped off to nearly zero.

When the shift supervisor came out, he told us that our shift was being eliminated until the slowdown was over. That was bad enough, but then he said that the company was short on cash and we wouldn't be able to get our severance pay until later.

It had only been two weeks since the crash, and I was out of a job, had no money, and had a wife and two kids to feed. When I came home in the middle of the day, Mary guessed what had happened.

"You lost your job, didn't you?" she asked.

"Not really," I told her, trying to ease the burden some. "It's just that orders are down, so they're furloughing our shift. You know they've done that before."

Mary didn't say anything, but I knew I wasn't fooling her. She just turned back to her ironing. "What about your severance pay?" she asked without looking at me.

"The supervisor said it would be a little while before we could get it. He said the company is short on cash right now, but it shouldn't be too long." I added the last part even though I knew she wouldn't believe it any more than I did. I thought it might give her something to hang onto.

In the three weeks that followed, I looked everywhere for a job—any job. But there weren't any jobs in Detroit. Almost every business in the city was tied to the car companies, and when they slowed down, everything slowed down.

Our food supply dwindled and things got critical. We couldn't expect much help, even from our friends at church. Most of them were in the same fix as us, or worse. The pastor did set up a food pantry in the church where anyone who had extra could share with those who had needs, and thank God for that! At least we were able to eat, even if it meant eating mostly beans for a while. I still believed what was happening was temporary. *A whole country can't just shut down,* I kept telling myself.

For the next eight months, I hopped rides from one town to the next, looking for any kind of work. But everywhere I went there were a hundred men ahead of me.

We missed the next month's mortgage payment, and a week later we got a notice from the bank saying we needed to pay up or vacate the premises.

"How can the bank do that?" Mary asked me angrily. "We can't get our money out, but they can tell us to move out of our home?"

I wasn't sure how the bank could do that either, but since it wasn't open anymore I couldn't even talk to anyone about it. A week later a man knocked on the door. Handing me an eviction notice, he said if we didn't vacate within the week he would be back with the police to put us out.

"But where will we go?" I shouted at him through the screen door. "We don't have any money, and the bank is closed!"

"I can't help you, mister," he replied without emotion. "I just serve the papers for the court. You'll have to get a lawyer and talk to the judge."

I knew we couldn't do that. I didn't have enough money for bus fare, much less to pay a lawyer. So we packed up what we could carry and got ready to move.

The church had set up a temporary shelter because so many families had lost their homes. We stayed there for nearly three weeks, until another couple offered to let us stay with them. The husband worked for the railroad so he still had a job, although his pay had been cut in half.

I knew I had to find work, and there just wasn't any in Detroit, so I had to go where there was work. My problem was that I didn't have any money and no real prospects of getting any.

The railroad engineer we were staying with mentioned that a lot of men were hitching rides on box cars to search for work. He said the railroad officials had tried to stop them, but there were just too many. "As long as you don't get on or off in the rail yards, the engineers will look the other way," he said. The next day I hopped a ride on a south-bound freight. Someone had said there was work in Florida.

For the next eight months, I hopped rides from one town to the next, looking for any kind of work, but everywhere I went there were a hundred men ahead of me. Desperate men stood on street corners selling apples or begging just to feed their families.

I spent nights in makeshift camps with other men looking for work. Some had given up already and made their way by stealing what they could to survive. Being a Christian, I knew the Lord wouldn't approve of such things.

I picked up a few odd jobs here and there—enough to keep body and soul together but not enough to help Mary and our kids much (our third child had been born by then).

It was almost a year before I finally got a regular job as a gardener at a mansion in Palm Beach. It didn't pay much, but it did come with a small cottage (as the owner called it). A year earlier I would have called it a shack.

I lived like slaves must have lived a hundred years earlier. What money I made went mostly for food, with a little to send back to the family. I earned about thirty cents a day, when I was paid at all. I worked from sunup to sundown, keeping up the grounds of a politician's winter residence. Even now, I still remember that big house sitting empty most of the year, while I slept in a run-down shack, fighting off blood-thirsty mosquitoes.

> *If I could advise the younger genera-*
> *tion, I'd say, "Believe only half of*
> *what you read about the economy*
> *and none of what you hear."*

Finally in 1934 the economy in Florida had improved enough for me to get a job selling insurance door-to-door on commission. It amazed me how so many people I called on had plenty of money, when most families were living hand-to-mouth. Once I hit on the idea of convincing the rich that insurance was a way for them to protect their money against another crash, things started to go pretty well for me.

By 1936 I was able to bring Mary and the boys down to Florida. I decided it was time to give up my caretaker job. I had kept it even though I was making a pretty good living selling insurance. I guess the Depression had left such an impact on me that I hesitated to give up a sure job for one where I didn't know if I'd sell anything from day to day. But once I had some of those rich customers telling their friends about me, business really picked up.

To this day, I still remember the "hobo" camps where a bunch of us would sit around a fire and talk about the "good ol' days" when we had jobs. No matter how good things got in later years, I continued to remind myself how bad they had been and could be again, so I always tucked something away in a secret place. I never needed it, but I guess it's like a fire insurance policy; it's there, just in case. . . .

If I could advise the younger generation, I'd say, "Believe only half of what you read about the economy and none of what you hear." By the time my generation knew we had a problem, it was too late to do anything about it. We thought we had all the answers too, but what we found out was that when the chips were down, the politicians still had their jobs; we didn't.

Bill retired in 1973 after having operated a highly profitable insurance business for nearly forty years. Until his death in 1984, he was involved in a major effort to eliminate government waste and warn Americans about the dangers of excessive debt.

The legacy of the "New Deal" was the rise of the federal government as the protector of the economy against the "capitalists."

From the modest beginnings of a $60 billion allocation of tax dollars to help unemployed Americans during the Depression, the federal government now spends $300 billion annually on subsidies to all classes of its citizens.

With the best of intentions, America's political leaders paved the way for the destruction of the soundest economy in the world. As Sir Winston Churchill once said, "the road to hell is paved with good intentions."

5
The Seeds of Destruction

The Great Depression actually ended with the United States' entry into World War II. There is no evidence that the measures taken by the New Deal administration actually did anything to shorten the Depression. Obviously they did help the plight of Americans suffering from the effects of a decade-long depression. I believe history will reflect that the short-range benefits given to the thirties' generation were provided at the expense of future generations. There is one certainty: The function of the federal government as a provider was established permanently.

World War II provided the impetus to solidify the government's role as the nation's chief economic architect. For nearly five years Franklin Roosevelt was in total control of the country. Survival necessitated strong leadership, and Roosevelt was not one to shirk that role.

Coming out of the war, there was a tremendous need to reintegrate the GIs into American society without disrupting the entire economy. The plan that was instituted was dubbed the "GI Bill." This law empowered the government to provide college grants to servicemen (and women), fund new housing under the Veteran's Administration Loan Act, and expand business in Europe through the use of loans to both allies and former enemies through the Marshall Plan. The federal government went into the development business in a big way.

> *Perhaps the most significant economic change of the second half of the twentieth century was the discovery of instant prosperity (called credit) by millions of American families.*

Logically speaking, the debts incurred during the war should have been paid off immediately after the hostilities ended. But with the expanded role of government, the surpluses were diverted into expanding U.S. influence at home and abroad instead. With the expansion of the Farm Credit Bureau, the Small Business Administration, the Veteran's Administration, and on and on, the country prospered in an unprecedented postwar boom.

Billions went into educating GIs and their spouses, as well as providing low-interest loans to house them. As the FHA program was expanded to provide low-cost financing to nonveterans, America went on a building boom. No one questioned the wisdom of the government-backed expansion. After all, taxes were low, interest rates were low, inflation was a modest one-half percent per year, and business was booming. Eisenhower was elected president and Americans thought prosperity was their God-given heritage.

Perhaps the most significant economic change of the second half of the twentieth century was the discovery of instant prosperity (called credit) by millions of American families. Since the Great Depression, most Americans had been weaned from the use of credit: some because of bitter memories, others because the bankers simply knew better than to lend money to people who could ill-afford it. Credit was available during the fifties but was limited primarily to home mortgages and some short-term car loans. During the sixties, loans for almost everything—from college tuition to television sets—burst onto the scene.

The federal government, after running budget surpluses during the Eisenhower administration, began its disastrous experiment with massive entitlement programs. If the Kennedy era could be dubbed "the space explosion," the Johnson era must be dubbed "the deficit explosion."

In his famous inaugural address, President Kennedy said, "Ask not what your country can do for you. . . ." At that time those with their hands in Uncle Sam's pockets numbered *only* about twenty-two million. In the next decade, that number would swell to almost 160 million.

President Lyndon Johnson was consumed by two strategies that would prove to be the most costly in American history: the protection of South Vietnam, and massive federal transfers to the "war on poverty."

Perhaps the economy could have absorbed either of these at any given time. We were, after all, the most prosperous nation on earth, with a trade surplus in almost every area of business. But not even the U.S. economy could swallow $100 billion of war costs and nearly $500 billion in welfare transfers in a five-year period without either some sizable tax increases or huge deficits. The federal government opted to increase both.

In the early sixties, average-income families paid about 7 percent of their income in direct taxes. They also spent about 15 percent of their disposable income on interest payments (primarily home mortgages).

By 1969 they were paying 14 percent of their incomes in taxes and spending 22 percent on interest. The amounts were still manageable but growing faster than incomes.

In 1963 the federal government collected approximately $107 billion in income taxes. By 1970 it was collecting more than $187 billion, an increase of some 42 percent, while incomes went up an average of 12 percent. Still, things weren't all that bad economically for most Americans. There were periodic bouts with recession, but essentially the period from 1961 to 1970 was the longest sustained period of economic growth in the history of the nation.

By the late sixties, many Americans who had lived through the Great Depression were leaving the work force and retiring to a stable, relatively noninflationary economy.

If the debt had been dealt with swiftly and aggressively, it could have been controlled or even eliminated. But Americans had no such mentality in the seventies, nor did their elected officials.

Interest rates had risen from approximately 4 percent in 1960 to about 6 percent by 1970—nothing to be alarmed about for the average home buyer. Besides, the "baby boomers" of the postwar era were coming into the mainstream, and they needed homes and cars, as well as a variety of other consumer goods. The sixties may have been tumultuous times politically, but economically the country was still on a roll.

A few prophets of doom continued the warnings about too much debt and too much government in the economy; but in large part, their warnings fell on deaf ears. Poverty was due to be eliminated by the mid-seventies; people were bored by men on the moon; and Watergate had not yet tarnished President Nixon's administration.

THE SEVENTIES

What few Americans realized was that the seeds from the New Deal were just beginning to germinate in the economy. The aggregate national debt had grown from $22 billion in 1932 to just under $400 billion by 1970. By 1979 the debt had doubled to $800 billion.

The difficulty with a debt that doubles in ten years is that the interest compounds to the point that it can no longer be paid out of current revenues. Once the interest itself is debt financed, the compounding accelerates.

If the debt had been dealt with swiftly and aggressively, it could have been controlled or even eliminated. But Americans had no such mentality in the seventies, nor did their elected officials. Tax revenues could never sustain the level of growth Americans were used to—not and still fulfill the Great Society's goals too. So by 1970 the die was cast for a debt-run economy in which the deficits of the past would seem minuscule in comparison. Instead of millions, we would hear of a deficit in the billions. Later the billions would aggregate to trillions.

Perhaps it would be helpful to use an analogy to the amounts of money we're discussing.

- A *million* dollars in tightly bound $1,000 bills would produce a stack four inches high.

- A *billion* dollars in tightly bound $1,000 bills would produce a stack about three hundred feet high.

- A *trillion* dollars in tightly bound $1,000 bills would produce a stack nearly *sixty-three miles* high!

Sometimes it's too easy to lose sight of what some of these numbers really mean. With budget deficits of only $3 billion a year in 1970 (actually a surplus if Social Security funds are taken into account), the Federal government went on a debt-funded spending binge. This was not to combat a depression or to oppose an invading army. It was a social experiment run amok with nearly 80 percent of all Americans eventually taking some form of government subsidy. We were literally mortgaging future generations to feed our indulgences. The traditional family suffered greatly as mothers went to work to help fund the family's debt and tax payments. The great wealth transfers of the 1920s were under way once again. Only this time even the federal government would mortgage the country.

Government strategies of the seventies failed to take into account two critical factors: the deficits would eventually translate into higher inflation and the compounding interest on the national debt would create even greater deficits.

The total federal debt increased by approximately $35 billion from 1950 to 1960 and by $90 billion from 1960 to 1970. But it would climb by *$600 billion* by 1980! But I'm getting ahead of myself in the logical progression of our economy.

In a futile attempt to control the "rampant" inflation of 1971 (4.3 percent), President Nixon ordered wage and price controls on the economy. No sooner were the controls in place than the political "negotiating" began. Those groups with the most lobbyists, or the biggest campaign contributors, began to receive special compensation. Within a few months, the only controls remaining were on the wages of average Americans. Wisely the controls were dropped altogether when the "victory" over inflation was proclaimed.

Then in 1973, the Arab oil embargo shocked most Americans into the realization that we were vulnerable too. Gas prices increased dramatically, climbing from forty cents per gallon to just over ninety cents, thus bringing inflation back onto center stage and paving the way for the fuel-efficient Japanese cars to reach into the American market in a big way.

Prices of virtually all consumer items inflated rapidly. It was as if the pent-up prices from the earlier controls broke loose and swept aside everything in their wake. Our nation started a spending binge that paralleled that of the 1910-to-1920 era, only this time it was amplified by the government's deficit spending as well.

Inflation creates a unique attitude in most people: a buy-now mentality.

During the four years of the Carter administration, the national debt increased by nearly $250 billion—an unparalleled amount prior to that time. But also inflation roared to life, sending price increases into the double digits annually. Here we get a brief but revealing glimpse at a hyperinflationary economy in the U.S.

By early 1979, inflation was running at nearly 12 percent per year. This was relatively minor compared to many other industrialized nations at that time. Israel's inflation rate was nearly 80 percent; England's was 20+ percent; Germany's was as high as 30 percent. But in the U.S. we were used to spending what we wanted with little or no economic consequences. Americans responded to double-digit inflation by demanding that the government do something about it.

The primary tool the administration decided to use to combat inflation was a decrease in the money supply. Not wishing to repeat the mistakes of the Nixon administration with wage and price controls, President Carter had few other choices.

The method by which the Federal Reserve manipulates the available money supply is either an increase or decrease in the amount of credit available. To reduce the money supply, the Fed raises interest rates, which makes borrowing more costly. As the cost of credit goes up, more and more potential borrowers drop out. Since we are an economy run almost exclusively on credit now, consumer buying slows and, hopefully, so does inflation. This was one of the controls established during the Roosevelt era.

In spite of all the "controls" installed by the New Deal, the primary steering mechanism in the economy still remains public confidence. Unfortunately, the public had lost its confidence in the Carter administration because of several politically devastating events: the Panama Canal treaty, the Iranian hostage situation, and the Vietnam war legacy that President Carter inherited.

As a result, the only real effect the increased interest rates had was a slowdown in economic growth. The economy entered a new phase not seen before—"stagflation": a condition in which the economy is stagnant while inflation is still rising. Effectively we got the worst of two worlds—inflation and recession.

Inflation creates a unique attitude in most people: a buy-now mentality. As the value of their money declines, consumers are motivated to buy commodities before the prices go higher. Young couples see their dream homes slipping away, so they extend beyond what normally would be prudent to buy that home. Investors see their paper assets eroding, so they rush out to buy "real" assets, such as land, buildings, precious metals, and the like.

The late seventies and early eighties were such times. Almost anything that could be used as an inflation hedge was purchased. People who should have known better were buying assets at greatly inflated values, believing that inflation was here to stay.

I need to digress again to explain something about inflation. Inflation is caused by one primary factor: an artificial increase in the money supply. Higher prices in an economy are a symptom, not the problem.

Allow me to illustrate. If all currency were tied to a fixed asset, such as gold, no additional money could be circulated without an equivalent increase in the amount of gold held in reserve. Since gold is relatively scarce and costly to mine, it cannot be increased rapidly. Therefore, the total currency in circulation is relatively constant when tied to the gold supply.

Individual commodities, such as coffee, can go up in price because of demand, but with a fixed amount of currency in circulation, if coffee goes up in price, something else must come down. In other words, consumers must make a choice of buying coffee at the sacrifice of some other commodity, such as sugar. Overall there is no increase in commodity prices; hence, no inflation.

Obviously there can be gradual price increases as the supply of gold is expanded, but these would be long-term, not sudden, increases.

But take the currency off of any fixed commodity standard and see what can happen. Let's assume that the amount of currency available is regulated only by the wishes of a small group of economists who regularly put more money into circulation as they deem it necessary to keep the economy stimulated (as is true with the Fed).

Now suppose the price of coffee goes up as consumers discover its great merits. But instead of allowing another commodity (sugar in our previous example) to decrease (because sugar is produced in the district of an influential congressman), the Fed simply creates more money to fund the increased price of coffee.

The result is an overall price increase in the economy that **is** more or less permanent. The "more or less" is determined by whether or not the Fed makes the currency expansion permanent.

Obviously the mechanics by which our currency is inflated is more complex than I presented, but I trust you can see the big picture.

Inflation of the money supply is precisely why the New Deal administration removed our money from the gold standard and, later, why President Nixon removed even our coins from the silver standard. The government economists now have created a mechanism whereby they can regulate the currency as they deem necessary. The result? Inflation.

WHY INFLATION DECLINED IN THE EIGHTIES

Actually, inflation did not decline in the eighties; it simply resumed the normal upward trend established before the rampant price increases of the seventies.

When Ronald Reagan became president, he brought into the office something that had been lacking in the previous three administrations: confidence. His programs were innovative (to be sure), and he was an eloquent orator. Simply put, Americans (in general) trusted his leadership.

> *What makes our government's debt
> so dangerous is that we are in debt
> beyond our total asset value. In other
> words, we are actuarily broke.*

As a result, the tough measures he adopted to choke off inflation were accepted as necessary. Also, since most Americans had confidence in his ability to do what he said, they lowered their panic level and stopped the run on real assets. Inflation quieted down to a mere 6 percent per year. What would have been unthinkable inflation in 1960 became "the good ol' days" in 1983.

"Reaganomics" instituted sweeping tax cuts, particularly for the upper-income taxpayers. The Reagan advisers assessed (correctly I believe) that more money in the hands of those with a surplus would be reinvested in the economy. The U.S. economy boomed for nearly eight years, but President Reagan left the White House having bloated our economy with debt. The largest deficits in the history of any economy (nearly $2.2 *trillion*) were accumulated during the longest period of uninterrupted economic growth.

THE X FACTOR: DEBT

The one factor we have not discussed yet is the three-dimensional aspect of our debt. We often think of "the debt" only in terms of our government when, in reality, that is one side of the three-sided debt issue: federal, consumer, and state.

THE NATIONAL DEBT

It is not new for our government or any other to borrow money. Most governments do so when in a crisis, such as a war. What is unique today is that our government borrows during good times and bad, during war and peace alike. But what makes our government's debt so dangerous is that we are in debt beyond our total asset value. In other words, we are actuarily broke.

The average taxpayer's "contribution" to the federal budget (based on an annual income of $38,000) operates our government for approximately 1.5 tenths of one second.

Unfortunately, there seems to be no thought of ever trying to repay the debt. In truth, our government cannot even pay the *interest* on its debt, unless it does so through additional borrowing. The media present countries like Mexico, Brazil, and Argentina as so-called "banana" republics because they must borrow to pay the interest on their debts. But who would have ever believed this was possible for the world's largest economy?

The graph below shows the growth of the federal debt since 1960. The projections through the year 2000 are taken from the president's Private Sector Survey on Cost Control, commissioned by President Reagan. Anyone who reads this graph and is not alarmed by the economic consequences for our nation, should enroll in Economics 101.

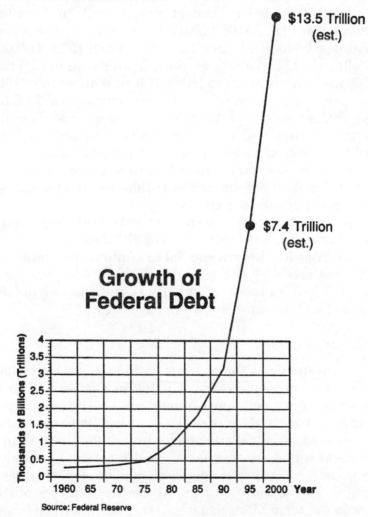

$13.5 Trillion (est.)

$7.4 Trillion (est.)

Growth of Federal Debt

Thousands of Billions (Trillions)

1960 65 70 75 80 85 90 95 2000 **Year**

Source: Federal Reserve

I personally believe these estimates to be on the conservative side. It is very possible that the federal debt could reach *$20 trillion* by the year 2000. At an interest rate of just 10 percent,

Americans would be paying $2 trillion a year in interest! That would leave about $1 trillion to operate the country, assuming that all Americans were being taxed at a 50 percent rate.

As of 1991, the "on budget" interest payment consumes 17 percent of all tax revenues. By the year 2000, the most conservative estimates place it at 50 percent of tax revenues.

In 1991 the federal budget was one trillion three hundred billion dollars ($1,300,000,000,000). In addition, the government spent nearly another three hundred billion ($300,000,000,000) in "off-budget" expenditures. Such figures tend to lose their significance to most of us, so let's put it in manageable "bites." At this spending level the federal government spends $4.6 billion a day! That amounts to $195 million an hour, or $3.25 million every minute, day and night. The average taxpayer's "contribution" to the federal budget (based on an annual income of $38,000) operates our government for approximately one-seventh of one second. Think about that the next time you read about how the government spends *our* money.

In 1960 the average taxpayer worked 36 days to pay all of his or her taxes. As of 1991, it takes 121 days.

In order for the government to continue to operate, it must either cut spending, increase revenues, or find another "fix." I believe it is this other "fix" that represents danger to our economy, as I will demonstrate later.

CONSUMER DEBT

As dramatic as the increase in the national debt has been since the depression years, it pales in comparison to the increase in consumer debt. Americans are literally consuming their asset base and transferring their wealth to the lenders.

As we saw in the latter stages before the Great Depression, there was a massive transfer of wealth via debt to lenders. Today there is an even more massive transfer of wealth leaving the country. This is more ominous since the transfers often come back in the form of foreign ownership of American businesses. In 1983 the Japanese invested $1 billion in the U.S. In 1985 they invested $6.5 billion. In 1986 it was $12 billion. In 1990 their investments were estimated to be $65 billion. They are collecting their profits and buying out America. If this trend continues at the same rate through the end of the decade, the Japanese alone will control 40 percent of all U.S. manufacturing and commercial property.

During the Great Depression it was in the interests of lenders (mostly bankers) to support the American economy. That will not necessarily be the case in the next depression. When push comes to shove (so to speak), the foreign lenders' interests will lie primarily with their own countries and in maintaining jobs for their people. With our government dependent on foreign loans for nearly half of its deficit spending, there is little that could be done to protect the interests of American workers.

Americans are living in an inflated economy created by the use of borrowed money. Since the early sixties, virtually all major assets have been purchased on credit. Since the mid-seventies, even consumer goods have been acquired on credit via the use of credit cards and equity loans.

Most American families, in spite of their outward appearance of affluence, live on the brink of economic disaster. They have little or no savings to fall back on in difficult times and now are borrowing against the equity in their homes to buy nonessential goods. If the value of their homes falls during an economic downturn, both the borrowers and the lenders are going to be in real trouble. The following charts give a graphic picture of where the average American is economically.

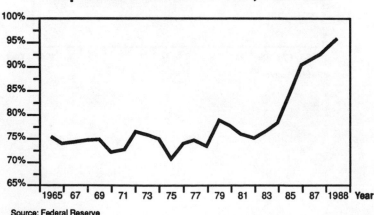

Outstanding Household Debt Relative to Disposable Personal Income, 1965-1988

Source: Federal Reserve

As you can see, the ratio of household debt to disposable income rose dramatically after 1983. Simply put, Americans borrowed their way into prosperity.

The next graph demonstrates even more dramatically the trend in consumer borrowing. Americans are rapidly consuming all their available equity. In essence, they are transferring their wealth to relatively few lenders, who then lend it to the government, who then pays it to foreign investors.

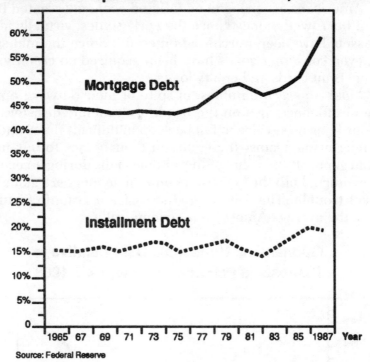

Home Mortgage Debt and Consumer Installment Debt Relative to Disposable Personal Income, 1965-1987

Source: Federal Reserve

This last graph indicates the source of the money that has funded the credit binge of the eighties (and nineties). Americans were persuaded to use their last source of available equity: their homes. When the tax laws were changed in 1986 to disallow interest deductions on all but home loans, the shift to equity lines of credit was clearly evident. One has to wonder if the law was changed specifically for this purpose. Without a new line of credit, the economy might well have slowed dramatically. The question is: Where will the next financial "rabbit" come from?

Home Mortgage Debt and Consumer Installment Debt Relative to Total Household Liabilities, 1965-1987

Source: Federal Reserve

STATE DEBT

Anyone who reads the newspapers or watches the evening news knows that many states are in severe financial trouble. The same abuses that we see at the federal level are evident on a smaller scale at the state (and local) level. It is astounding to

hear of state debts in the billions of dollars. It is even more astounding to hear about cities (like New York and Boston) with
debts in the billions. It's as if the whole public system has gone
insane. There is virtually no way these state governments can
sustain such huge debts, and there is no "politically acceptable"
way to repay them. With the taxpayers already struggling financially, higher taxes will push them to the brink of disaster, economically and emotionally.

Bear in mind that all of the debts owed by state and local
governments are loans made by people who live off the proceeds. If these governments default, the ripple will be felt
throughout the economy. With our economy teetering on the
edge of disaster already, any ripple could swamp it. Any economy lives or dies on the basis of public confidence. Lose that
confidence, and the system crashes.

As the following graph demonstrates, the growth of nonfed-
eral public debt has reached the epidemic level. We will certainly see many municipalities, and perhaps even some states
appealing to the courts for bankruptcy protection. That will be
an interesting study in constitutional law—to see if the federal
bankruptcy act extends to local governments.

WHAT'S NEXT?

I trust that I neither bored you nor panicked you with all
the details on debt in America, but it is the key to understanding
the future direction of our economy.

As I said earlier, those who fail to learn from the past are
doomed to repeat it. You'd think that just a little more than six
decades after the most severe depression in U.S. history, we
would remember the lessons learned: you can't spend more
than you make forever and not pay the price, and when the bot-
tom falls out it is the *lenders* who will be protected, not the
borrowers.

God's Word gives us a clear indication that this principle
has endured for more than three thousand years. For as Proverbs 22:7 says, "The rich rules over the poor, And the borrower
becomes the lender's slave."

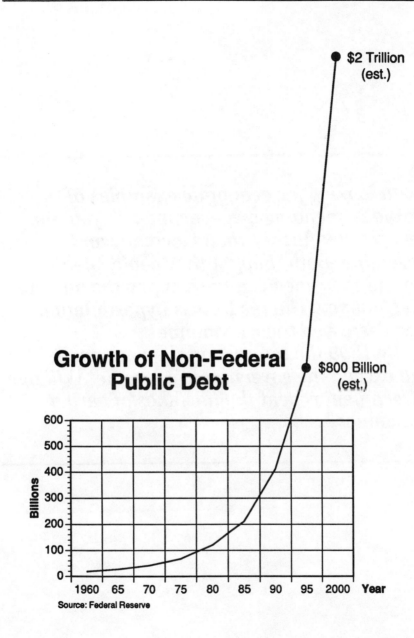

$2 Trillion (est.)

Growth of Non-Federal Public Debt

$800 Billion (est.)

Billions

600
500
400
300
200
100
0

1960   65   70   75   80   85   90   95   2000   **Year**

Source: Federal Reserve

In looking for economic examples of frivolous spending by governments, you don't have to look further than Germany and Argentina. Both thought they could spend beyond their means and then pay the bill with "fiat" money. The result was hyperinflation that destroyed their economies.

By 1999 the interest on the national debt will exceed the government's income. Will our government repeat the mistakes of earlier economies?

6
Germany and Argentina: Examples to Avoid

THE LESSONS OF GERMANY

As a history buff, I try to recognize parallels between past events and current trends. At first glance, the parallels between 1990 America and 1918 Germany may not be obvious, but I believe there are many.

Germany, before the humiliating defeat in Europe, had an economy that was the envy of all Europe. However, after World War I, in the wake of the treaty at Versailles, the German government was required to make economic reparations to her European neighbors. To do so required transferring most of Germany's gold reserves to France and England. That left the German deutschemark (called reichsmark from 1925 to 1948) virtually stripped of any hard currency to support it.

Additionally, Germany had chronic unemployment because so much of her industry had been dismantled and removed to France and Belgium after the Allies overran the country. The government was put in the compromising position of finding it necessary to support the unemployed or risk rebellion in the cities during a very difficult economic time. This required a sizeable portion of the German budget to be siphoned off into transfer payments at a time when the government could least afford it.

The "enlightened" philosophy was that currency should not be linked to precious metals anyway, since it allowed for no direct government control over the economy. This philosophy would eventually resurface in America during the "New Deal."

The debt payments to England and France for the war damage further stripped the country of needed operating capital, and Germany's main creditor, France, refused to budge on required payments. As one of the Proverbs says, "so the rich rule over the poor." Germany was faced with making some tough economic decisions, including the cessation of transfer payments (what we now call entitlements).

Instead, the government took the easier path of "monetizing" their currency. *Monetizing* is a polite economic term that means creating fiat (phony) money—sometimes called "funny money."

When the German government made the decision to print the money it needed, it was hailed by progressive economists as an enlightened move. The "enlightened" philosophy was that currency should not be linked to precious metals anyway, since it allowed for no direct government control over the economy. This philosophy would eventually resurface in America during the "New Deal."

It was assumed that by injecting a modest amount of new currency into the economy, only a modest amount of inflation would follow. Advocates of this plan assured the Kaiser that a modest amount of inflation would be manageable and would actually allow producers to reap more profits, thus helping to repay the country's debts with cheaper currency.

When the decision to print unsupported money was made, the value of the German currency was approximately four marks to the dollar. Almost immediately the currency was devalued to about nine marks per dollar, achieving the economists' desired effect: German exports were suddenly more competitive, and debts were effectively cut in half by inflation.

Inside Germany it was another matter altogether. Suddenly creditors saw their loans reduced by half, along with their buying power. They lobbied the government for equalization—meaning that all loans should be indexed to the devalued mark.

When a loan is indexed, it requires that the principal amount be increased by the rate of inflation (much as Social Security payments are now). So if the currency is devalued by 50 percent, outstanding loans double in value. This has the effect of passing the burden along to the borrowers, instead of the lenders.

The request was initially rejected, and effectively all debts, internal and external, were cut in half. All new lending in Germany ceased at this point. No lender was willing to risk another devaluation and lose a sizeable portion of his equity to inflation.

What had seemed like a windfall to the debtors soon became a nightmare. The Allies (with the exception of England) demanded that Germany pay its war debts in kind (real goods), rather than with the devalued German currency. To guarantee this, France occupied a portion of the Ruhr coal mining district. Coal was Germany's main export, and France was determined to get its fair share. Instead, German workers declared a passive strike, effectively cutting off Germany's only source of foreign currency.

To compensate for the lack of currency, the Reichsbank (the German equivalent of our Federal Reserve) authorized the printing of more currency. This would prove to be the downfall of the German economy and, ultimately, the Republic.

As I commented previously, when any government makes the decision to inflate its economy through debt, eventually it will be faced with more difficult decisions about how to repay that debt. As long as the debt is held by its own people, the solutions are somewhat easier because it is in their interests to maintain the system. When the debt is held by foreigners, however, there is no choice but to either pay up or risk losing the ability to trade with other nations. Inevitably the government is faced with three basic choices: default, raise taxes, or inflate the currency.

Germany could not easily raise taxes since a large portion of its population was out of work, and a default would mean economic disaster. So, against the warnings of economists like Dr. Ludwig Von Mises, the government chose to inflate.

Immediately the currency rate fell from 8.9 marks per dollar to 191 marks to the dollar. Inside Germany this devaluation effectively wiped out all the creditors. In addition, retirees who held government or bank bonds saw their assets devalued by 2000 percent in one day!

Once the cycle started, it was virtually impossible to control. The government overseers authorized the printing of more currency to compensate for the devaluation. At the same time, they attempted to establish price controls within Germany to help stabilize the economy. The effect was to punish the working class, while many of the industrialists shifted to the black market to sell their goods at much higher prices. And since most of these sales went untaxed, this further reduced the federal revenues.

---

*The net result of hyperinflation
was the dissolution of
the German government.*

In June of 1922 the currency rate dropped to 350 marks per dollar. By October it was 4,500 per dollar. Prices were changing so rapidly in the stores that merchants adopted an indexing system. The prices on the goods, which might be several days old, were multiplied by the devalued mark. For example, a can of beans with a price of ten marks stamped on it would be indexed by a factor of thirty, making the current price three hundred marks. As the currency prices changed, so did the food prices—

about every minute or so! Within a few months an equivalent can of beans would sell for more than one million marks!

Once hyperinflation struck Germany, bank loans were indexed to the currency devaluation. But since wages were not indexed, the loans escalated far beyond the average worker's ability to repay them. Most average-income workers lost everything they owned. This massive shift of wealth would later pave the way for the National Socialist German Worker's Party (Nazis) to grasp power. The wealthy got wealthier, and the middle class got wiped out.

By January of 1923 the exchange rate was 18,000 marks per dollar. Prices changed while customers stood in long checkout lines. All the merchandise was cleaned out of the stores as soon as it was unloaded. In anticipation of the higher prices when they reordered, merchants would often mark their goods up several thousand percent higher than the "legal" daily limit.

Even so, it was not enough, and many small merchants failed, leaving the struggling, average-income workers with no place to buy except the black market, where a loaf of bread might sell for 100,000 marks—the equivalent of a month's wages at the time.

By October the currency exchange rate fell to 4.2 *trillion* marks per dollar! The deutschemark became worthless. Lifetimes of savings were wiped out, and the only form of trade for most Germans was barter. The mark became so worthless that the paper it was printed on was actually more valuable than the currency itself. So, instead of printing more currency, the Reichsbank simply issued stamps that could be pasted over existing bills.

I have a 1923 German bill that began with a value of 10,000 marks. The last stamp applied revalued it to three billion!

The net result of hyperinflation was the dissolution of the German government. After the collapse of the economy, Germans turned to socialism, believing that the free-enterprise system had failed them. When the depression of 1929 struck, Germany still had not recovered from the devastating effects of the earlier collapse. An obscure ex-Army corporal by the name of Adolf Hitler took over the government with the promise of "economic prosperity."

ARGENTINA: A MORE RECENT EXAMPLE

Often Americans think of Argentina as a small South American country whose economy is based mainly on ranching. But in 1940 Argentina was one of the world's fastest developing countries. In fact, it was the fifth largest exporter in the world. It was (and is) a country with great natural resources and the potential to become a world leader.

The example of Argentina is a study in what *not* to do to an economy. The Argentine leaders were greatly influenced by American economists who followed the theory known as Keynesian Economics. To refresh your memory, this is the philosophy that the central government should control the economy for the "good" of the workers. To implement Keynesian economics requires both a strong central monetary system, such as the Federal Reserve, and the ability to inflate the currency when necessary.

Most bureaucracies operate on the old formula of "more money in—more money out."

In the early seventies Argentina, as well as many other developing countries, went on an aggressive modernization program, hoping to regain its pre–World War II status. To do so the Argentine government borrowed huge sums of money from foreign banks, especially those in the United States.

By 1980 their debt was $44 billion—nearly matching their GNP and requiring half of the government's income just to service the interest on the debt. Each successive year required more loans to keep the interest payments current. By the mid-eighties the international loan market began to dry up as lenders sensed a pending Argentine default. The Argentine government was faced with three choices: default, raise taxes, or inflate the currency.

As with most politicians who have sold their people on the role of the government as "the great provider," it is very difficult to pare back. In our country the politicians might face an angry electorate. In Argentina they might well have faced a firing squad.

If Argentina had simply defaulted on its debts, virtually all access to any additional loans would have been cut off. With an economy just beginning to emerge again, that would have resulted in some severe and immediate cutbacks. Perhaps in the long run, that track would have been better for the people, but few politicians operate in the "long run" today, so that option was discarded.

The second option of tax increases (and spending cutbacks) would seem the most logical approach. After all, that's what is expected of individuals when they overspend their own budgets, isn't it? But Argentina already had a tax rate of over 40 percent and a government that was spending money faster than the people could make it. Most bureaucracies operate on the old formula of "more money in—more money out."

Instead, the Argentine government, just as the Germans did some sixty years earlier, opted for the easy way out and began to inflate its currency. Simply put, they printed the money they needed.

In December 1989, to compensate for the new money that was being printed, the government devalued the Argentine currency (the austral) by 35 percent. On the black market, however, the austral dropped by an additional 50 percent, reflecting its true value. The official government valuation was 950 australs to the dollar; the rate anyone would actually accept was 1,500, but even that wouldn't last very long.

The government estimated that inflation would increase about 20 percent as a result of their actions. Instead it rose by nearly 700 percent! The middle class in Argentina was rapidly being wiped out. Retirees, pensioners, and those living on fixed incomes were destitute in less than a month.

In an effort to control the rampant inflation, the government froze prices on public services such as buses, hospitals, and utilities. But to cover the rising costs of imported goods, they had to print more money.

Within six months of printing the first currency, inflation accelerated to just under 100 percent per month! That meant the average Argentinean lost half of his buying power every single month. Before another six months had passed, the people of Argentina would look back on those times as "the good ol' days."

Prices in the open air markets of Buenos Aires soared as much as 100 percent *daily* as Argentineans rushed to buy all available food, anticipating greater inflation. Within one year of printing the first worthless currency, all savings were wiped out, and the only possible form of trade was barter (or dollars, which were illegal to own then). The Argentine economy was collapsing, and no other country would accept australs in payment for anything.

To encourage Argentineans to "save" and not convert their money into dollars on the black market, banks were directed to raise their interest rates to 600 percent per year. But with the annual inflation rate estimated at 2,000 percent, the interest hike did little to entice those with surpluses to leave them in the banks. There was a hemorrhage of assets leaving Argentina for other countries as the wealthy traded land, businesses, and whatever else they had for foreign currency. Land speculators were doing a booming business with wealthy Argentineans until they discovered that they were trading real assets for worthless paper. They quickly shifted their strategy, selling the land to foreign investors who would pay in other currencies.

One of the economic possibilities
for the United States studied
by the Grace Commission was
that of hyperinflation.

By January of 1990 the annualized inflation rate was about 5,600 percent. Prices tripled while Argentineans slept. Millions were made in one black market trade, and then lost on the next one. That didn't provide much of an incentive to save. An American businessman visiting Argentina asked his Argentine counterpart if he should take a cab or a bus to their luncheon. "Take a cab," his associate quipped. "You don't have to pay until you get there, so it's cheaper." That mentality was more than just a joke in Argentina. All paper currency was converted into real assets as quickly as possible.

In an effort to gain at least some degree of control over inflation, the government (at the insistence of the World Bank) established the equivalent of martial law over the economy. The currency was frozen and the printing of any new money was forbidden; wages and prices were frozen; black marketing was punishable by long prison sentences; and so on. This helped to establish some semblance of sanity in an insane system, and by early 1991 inflation was reduced to a mere 300 percent per year.

SWIFT INFLATION

Inflation does not have to creep into an economy, as the examples of both Argentina and Brazil demonstrate. When Argentina's annual budget deficit rose from 5 percent of their gross national product (about where the United States is in 1991) to 8 percent, inflation jumped from 4 percent per month to over 50 percent—in less than one year!

In Brazil, when the annual budget deficit reached 8 percent of the GNP, the inflation rate jumped from about 13 percent per month (considered modest in South America) to nearly 150 percent per month—in three days!

In 1984 President Reagan commissioned a panel of private citizens to review the federal budget and make recommendations on how to reduce the deficits. The study, under the direction of J. Peter Grace, was dubbed the Grace Commission. I will refer to that commission's report in subsequent chapters because it clearly reveals our economy's present and future conditions. One of the economic possibilities for the United States studied by the Grace Commission was that of hyperinflation. To get an accurate picture of what sparks hyperinflation (annual price increases of at least three digits), a committee selected by the Grace Commission did an extensive study of inflation in other countries. One of the principle figures in this study was Harry E. Figgie, Jr., chairman and chief executive officer of Figgie International, Inc., and a world-renowned industrialist.

While visiting Brazil, Argentina, Mexico, and Bolivia to evaluate their hyperinflation, Mr. Figgie was struck by the similar comments made by the more conservative members of their monetary policy groups.

In effect they all said something very similar: "What's wrong with the United States? You are on the same course that we were on—just several years behind us. Everything that we did wrong, you are doing wrong—only on a bigger scale. You have big budget deficits. You have a deficit in your balance of payments. You have allowed confidence in your currency to be eroded. You are dependent on foreign loans. You blame outsiders for your problems. Your businessmen call for more protectionism. And the exchange value of your currency is falling."

Their final comment to Mr. Figgie was, "Can't you tell your government to stop this madness before it's too late?"

Mr. Figgie's reply was, "I sure do hope so."

That was in 1985. Six years later the deficits are bigger, the balance of payments are worse, and the government has yet to implement more than a token amount of the Grace Commission's suggestions.

Mr. Figgie had an ominous word for Americans when he spoke before the League of Women Voters in July of 1990:

> There's never been a more critical time in our country than right now. There's never been a more critical issue than our budget deficits.
>
> This isn't a Democratic issue and it isn't a Republican issue. It's an American issue. We have perhaps five years left to deal with this problem through taxation and spending cuts, or we will pay the price others have paid. . . .
>
> More than 14 percent of our government's annual income now goes to pay foreigners' interest on our growing debt. By 1995, that amount will grow to nearly 25 percent.

This is an ominous warning from a respected financier who has no political "axe to grind." Later we will review some of the Grace Commission's more revealing predictions for the future of our economy.

It is interesting to note that many members of the Commission, as well as the report itself, came under great criticism by the economic liberals in Congress. The Commission members, who served at their own expense and paid all of their own staff, and whose committees were equally represented by Democrats and Republicans, were often accused of "partisan" politics—a term perfected in our Congress.

Everything in the world seems to go in cycles. We even keep track of time by the cycles of the earth and moon. But does the economy have dependable cycles that signal economic events? According to many cycle theorists, it does.

Cycle advocates generally agree that major economic downturns occur every sixty years or so. This would place the next depression around the turn of the century. Is this an inalterable event governed by laws as predictable as the law of gravity, or is it merely the logical conclusion of foolish actions?

7

Cycles of Depression

Much has been written about economic cycles in America. Some economists have even suggested that the cycles are so predictable they can be relied upon to a high degree for most economic planning.

Perhaps the most well-known of the twentieth-century cycle theorists was Russian economist N. D. Kondratieff. According to Dr. Kondratieff's theory, the economy consists of long waves of chaotic activity. The long waves are periods of economic change that include depressions, wars, inflation, and the like. These are demonstrated to occur approximately every fifty to sixty years.

The link between economic down cycles and the major wars is well documented. Throughout much of mankind's history, when the economy plunged into depression, one nation tried to dominate other nations—especially its neighbors—for its own economic benefit. Often during times of depression, despotic rulers rise to power with promises of a better life. When the economy does not progress the way they promise, they start a war to divert attention.

Kondratieff's observation of fifty- to sixty-year "cycles" is entirely plausible. As we can witness in our own economy, that seems to be about the time it takes for one generation to pass away and the next to repeat its mistakes. One would think that in our modern information era we could avoid the errors of our forefathers, but I assume many people in earlier generations must have thought the same thing.

> *There is sufficient data to prove that, from a historical perspective, the economy does go through periodic (and predictable) cycles.*

Enough changes are made in each successive generation so that those in charge believe they are smarter than the previous leaders. The 1929 generation had telephones, electric adding machines, even radios. I'm sure that because of those modern devices they thought they had a better handle on the economy than their predecessors did during the depression of 1893. They were completely confident that in 1929 the mistakes of the past would not be repeated.

The 1990s generation has computers with enormous information capacity; daily reports come from every corner of the globe; television keeps the American people updated (or confused); and the Federal Reserve keeps watch over the monetary system. With all these improvements, who could question our ability to avoid another economic calamity? Well, me for one. And eventually, I trust, you too.

THE CASE FOR CYCLES

There is sufficient data to prove that, from a historical perspective, the economy does go through periodic (and predictable) cycles. Approximately every fifty to sixty years since records have been kept (back to 1790), there have been major downturns lasting three years or longer. Traditionally these have been labeled major depressions. Punctuated between these major down cycles have been shorter downturns (recessions), lasting from a few months to as long as two years. A few have even lasted for as long as three years. What separated these "recessions" from the depressions was how long and how deep they were. Usually they were limited in intensity and did not endanger the stability of the overall economic system. The downturn (recession) of 1974-1976 is an example of this. Although it seemed severe to the people who lost their jobs, the recession did not threaten the overall stability of our economic system. The 1990-1991 recession fits this description also.

As the following chart shows, the cycles of the U.S. economy are not just random patterns. They appear regularly and at least somewhat predictably. The shorter recessions appear approximately every three to five years. The longer the interval between downturns, the more severe the eventual economic slump. The major downturns are just as reported—approximately every fifty to sixty years.

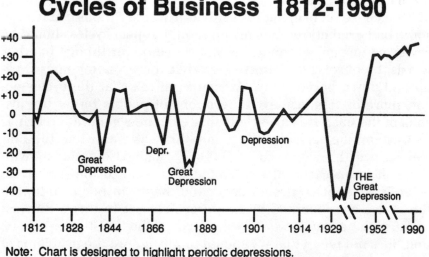

Cycles of Business 1812-1990

Note: Chart is designed to highlight periodic depressions.

A logical assumption would be to utilize this cycle record to predict economic activity in future years. And, to some extent, this can be done. Unfortunately all is not that clear. If a statistician looks long enough, he or she will find a cycle in almost everything, because basically all events are cyclical to some degree. The earth cycles the sun once a year, and the moon cycles the earth once a month. However, to presume this pattern is the same for every planetary body would yield some bad results. Each planet has its own cycle—randomly altered by the differing forces closest to it.

In the past decade we have dropped from the status of creditor nation to that of debtor nation.

Similarly, each economic era has its own differing forces that shape its cycle. If we were to fill in the missing economic activities in the previous chart, you would see that there is much more activity during some periods and less during others. Cycle-theory advocates sometimes treat this conflicting data as being of little consequence, but in reality these aberrations can lead to some bad predictions. It is my opinion that past cycles should be reviewed for major trends, but not relied on for timing. In other words, by observing them we see that the economy does cycle up and down periodically. We can even tell that the cycles occur, more or less, as new generations of people forget the lessons of the past. It is also clear that each new generation brings its own unique variables. Certainly this was true when the Bolsheviks overthrew the czar of Russia, bringing Communism with them. It is also true of the United States since the New Deal established the Keynesian economic theory in our country. So the cycles are modified by the forces closest to them. But just because the economy doesn't conform to the latest cycle theory, that does not mean that we should totally ignore the problems of the past either.

CHANGES IN THE CYCLES

The period of 1987 to 1989 paralleled the 1927 to 1929 era so closely it was astounding, even alarming. Even the most ardent admirer of the Keynesian economic theory could not deny the similarities. Because of this, several best-selling books were written about "the crash of 1990."

But the economy didn't crash in 1990. Instead, we entered a relatively short-lived (thus far) recession of moderate severity. As a result, many people (government economists among them) have concluded that the controls now in place are sufficient to avoid all future depressions. Such logic is both faulty and foolish.

In reality, the only conclusion that can be drawn is that we have the ability to delay the inevitable and lengthen the time between major cycles. The controls we have are adequate to alter, but not stop, the direction of our economy.

The strength of the U.S. economy is truly remarkable when some of the negatives against it are considered. For instance:

- Twenty percent of all Americans work directly for federal, state, and local governments and, as such, create no new goods and services.

- Eighty percent of all Americans now draw some form of government subsidy in the way of loans, grants, or direct transfer.

- Our currency is not backed by any fixed-value assets, has been inflated by huge amounts of debt, and yet is still the value standard throughout the world—at least for now.

Unfortunately, in the past decade we have dropped from the status of creditor nation to that of debtor nation. We have annual budget deficits in the hundreds of billions of dollars; we have a national debt that exceeds our government's total net worth; and the American taxpayer now works four months to pay federal taxes and a fifth month to pay state and local taxes.

Even with all our technology and material resources, we have not actually found a way to avoid the economic cycles— only delay them. If the cycle theory proves anything, it is that to delay the inevitable correction only makes the problem worse.

One of the better explanations of what happens when a normal economic cycle is broken was presented by Professor Ravi Batra in his book *The Great Depression of 1990.* Unfortunately, as the title might lead you to believe, Dr. Batra also predicted a depression in 1990. I personally believe the prediction was added more to sell books in 1989 than to pin a date on the next major depression. The information provided in the book is valid, even though the prediction wasn't.

Batra demonstrates conclusively that the U.S. economy has cycled through periods of "boom and bust" since the nation was founded, just as all other economies have. In other societies, the indicators are not as clear as they are in America, with our open society. Prior to the founding of our nation 200 years ago, most countries were governed by some form of dictatorship, as were the eastern European countries until the late 1980s. In a closed society, little information is provided about economic cycles. Also, the economy can be manipulated artificially until the whole system literally collapses. Russia, Europe, and China are classic examples of this. The evidence that the Russian leaders wanted their economy to appear stable is witnessed by the disappearance of Professor Kondratieff. Once his cycle theory was made public, showing the Russian economy also had its ups and downs, Kondratieff was sent to teach in Siberia, never to be seen or heard from again.

Prior to the collapse of communism in Russia and China, the people of those countries scarcely recognized the difference between the boom and bust cycles. The boom periods simply meant the government was able to spend more on the military, and the stores had two kinds of potatoes instead of just one.

Batra's information points out that the U.S. economy has experienced major down cycles approximately every thirty years. Interspersed between these major cycles were smaller cycles (recessions). The criteria he used to define a recession were a downturn of three years or less, with an unemployment rate of less than 9 percent. A depression, therefore, was defined as a downturn of more than three years, with an unemployment rate of greater than 9 percent. Certainly today we would readily agree that this would qualify as a depressed economy. If we had a downturn that lasted more than three years with 10 percent of the labor force unemployed, we would have business and personal bankruptcies on a scale never seen before in our history. In short, we are significantly more vulnerable to prolonged downturns than we were in previous generations.

Batra also points out that the severity of most of the *great depressions* (12 percent unemployment and 5 years or longer in duration) was determined primarily by whether or not a depression occurred every thirty years or every sixty years. Bear in mind that there is no mystical aspect to the cycles. They are the normal corrections for an imbalanced economy. Where the corrections are delayed because of war, excessive debt accumulation, or government manipulation, the next down cycle is more severe.

> *In the early sixties, no one would have believed our economy (or any other) could absorb nearly $4 trillion in debt and still survive.*

If Batra's observations are correct, and I can find no objective reason why they are not, then each additional decade the correction is delayed makes the prospect of a *Great Depression* more acute.

What has clouded the issue today is that since the 1920 depression we have had unusually long periods of prosperity, interrupted by relatively minor downturns. This is Keynesian economics operating to the fullest. It is an example of the government using the controls of a central bank, depositor insurance, and debt accumulation to stimulate and support the economy during both good times and bad.

I doubt that any rational economist truly understands the total effect that such controls can have on a huge economy such as ours. When I attended economics classes in the early sixties, no one would have believed our economy (or any other) could absorb nearly $4 trillion in debt and still survive. Nor would anyone have believed that the government could manage more than $300 billion in annual deficits. Simply put, the U.S. economy is a whole lot more resilient than anyone ever imagined, including Lord Keynes. The question is, how long can any economy survive under these conditions?

In the early 1980s I was teaching financial conferences around the country and felt compelled by the Lord to share my belief (then and now) that no economy can absorb forever the amount of debt that our economy is experiencing. But most people didn't want generalities. They wanted times and dates, so I was often asked, "How long until the economy collapses?"

At the time, I suggested the longest period I could conceive this huge transfer of wealth would continue—ten years. But ten years have come and gone and the economy still survives. We are deeper in debt than even the most liberal of liberals ever dreamed we would be, and yet we continue to operate in a somewhat "normal" fashion.

As you will see later, the actual deficits are almost twice as large as those admitted by the government. So why hasn't our economy collapsed? Because the American people still have confidence in "the system." The heart of the system depends on borrowing to fund the budget deficits each year. The interest on a $3 trillion debt amounts to $240 billion annually, or about 40 percent of all personal income taxes paid. When this debt swells to $20 trillion in nine years or so, the annual interest will be $1.6 trillion, or about 200 percent of all personal income taxes projected for that year (at a 33 percent rate).

Accurately predicting the precise time of a major economic downturn (great depression) is virtually impossible.

So how do we break out of this debt spiral? We don't. Unfortunately we have no choice but to continue with more of the same. It's as one of my economics professors liked to say: "He who rides on the back of a tiger cannot dismount."

The interest that most Americans are paying on their own debts should have transferred most of their wealth to the bankers and other lenders by now. The fact that a lot of it has been transferred can be seen in the large bank buildings in every city. But Uncle Sam, in the mode of Robin Hood, has been taking some of the earnings from the rich and giving it back to the poor by way of transfer payments. The transfer payments are not enough to keep them from being poor, but the payments are enough to allow them to continue participating in the economy. Slowly but surely, however, the middle class is being eliminated. The "poor" get federal subsidies for education, housing, health care, even food. The wealthy have enough to provide these benefits for themselves. The middle class borrow against the little equity they have remaining to pay for what they need.

We have another "Catch 22" in the transfer of wealth out of our country. As the national debt continues to grow, our dependence on foreign loans continues to mount. Eventually the interest leaving the country will exceed the government's tax revenues. Then a "solution" must be found.

A short-range solution will be more taxes. One recurring suggestion is to tax the "wealthy" more. The difficulty is that if all the income above $100,000 a year were taken from the wealthy, it would operate our government for only ten days! Also, stripping the wealthy of all their surpluses is a little like killing the goose that lays the golden eggs. The poor don't invest for the future. They need all they have just to live.

The second part of this Catch 22 is the danger of foreign investors not lending us the money we need. If they stop lending, then we must print the money (monetize the debt). When we begin this process, hyperinflation is certain to follow. So what do we do? It's a little like a cowboy in the old west riding his horse to death trying to avoid the Indians chasing him. He knows if he keeps on riding, his horse will eventually collapse. But he also knows if he stops, *he* will die. So he rides on, hoping for a miracle.

I have concluded that accurately predicting the precise time of a major economic downturn (great depression) is virtually impossible. Furthermore, until we get inside the "window of statistical probability," all attempts to establish a time is purely guesswork. The window of statistical probability occurs when the circumstances get so bad economically that no amount of further manipulation is possible to keep the economy going at a reasonably normal pace.

Let's assume this "window," where we can accurately determine what is going to happen in the economy, is one year. In other words, only when we get within one year of a major economic collapse will the indicators be clear. What we need to do is establish a template of these economic indicators (I will label them "cracks") and continue sliding it along the time line until the indicators line up. Then we will have an indication of the actual timing. It is much like making a template of a small section of a road map. You slide the template along the map until it matches a section on the full map. Then you can see where you are in the bigger picture.

One difficulty with our economic "template" is that, at best, it can provide only one year or less of warning. A second is, if the indicators are wrong, we may miss the "window" entirely.

I am not totally convinced that all the economic indicators signaling a depression are clear enough to make such a template. However, I do believe there are sufficient indicators available to give at least some warning. It is entirely possible that the economy has been manipulated by our government so long that an accurate long-term projection is not possible today. That's why so many of the cycle theorists have been wrong thus far. But these cycles can provide a reasonably accurate picture of what happened just prior to the great depressions of the past. Many of the same indicators should be present prior to the next one.

I have a friend in the commodities business who developed a computer model of most of the past cycles in the commodities market. Each of these cycles had slightly different but predictable patterns that occurred prior to a major upturn or downturn in the market. It seemed reasonable to assume that if he programmed all these factors into a computer and checked them daily he would be able to predict future trends in the commodities market.

Since there are tens of thousands of daily variables that can affect the price of commodities, it is impossible for humans to do this. But with the high-speed processing capabilities of modern computers, it is a simple task to check a million different variables every second if necessary. So my friend programmed all of the past data into his computer and then applied this very sophisticated program to the real commodities market. The result: It didn't work.

This perplexed him because when he applied the program to past events it worked perfectly. In other words, if he took all the data available prior to a known (major) market downturn and verified it against the data *just* prior to the event, his program signaled a warning. His quandary was, if it would work looking backward, why wouldn't it work looking forward?

Measuring from the end of the last great depression would place the next major depression in the year 2000.

The fact is, today the commodities market is subject to different factors than those seen in the past. For instance, the program failed to predict a major drop in soybean prices during the Falkland Islands' war between Argentina and England. Why? Because there had never been such a war before. Common sense said that soybean prices should have gone up since Argentina was a large exporter of soybeans at the time. Indeed, that is exactly what the program predicted, but since England overwhelmed Argentina in the brief skirmish, the market reacted favorably and soybean prices dropped.

So my friend went back to his computer and began to program some "what if" variables. He also realized the program would not be able to look very far into the future, because the variables became impossibly complicated. He asked the program to predict only the immediate reaction the market might take to circumstances around it; basically he built a "template."

The result is that he now has a program with an accuracy of 70 percent on short-range market reactions. Seventy percent may not sound all that great to a noncommodities dealer, but in the commodities business it is phenomenal.

The greatest discovery he made is that the program is over 90 percent accurate in predicting major market downturns. In the commodities business, it is more critical to avoid major downturns than to hit major upturns because the losses in one bad market can wipe out years of profits.

In the case of the economy, the same basic principle holds true: Avoiding one major depression is more important than profiting in ten growth periods.

THE SIXTY-YEAR CYCLES

From all the statistical data now available, I am convinced that the normal period between major down cycles (depressions) is in the sixty-year range. This is not an absolute by any means, and plus or minus 10 percent is six years, so flexibility is essential.

I also believe that the sixty-year period should be measured from the end of one major depression to the beginning of the next. Measuring from the end of the last great depression would place the next major depression in the year 2000 (plus or minus the variable). Only time will tell whether this is the correct timing or not. But if we can develop the sliding indicators (template), perhaps the next depression can be detected before it happens.

Spending beyond our means endangers our economic future. Debt prosperity is a fleeting illusion that is impossible to maintain. The use of credit doesn't eliminate a problem. It delays it and makes it worse.

The federal government now owes nearly $4 trillion, with virtually no way to repay the debt. By the year 2000, when the debt will be $20 trillion, just the interest alone will consume all the taxes paid by all Americans.

8

The Growth of Debt

Kenneth was from a long line of farmers. He inherited nearly 1,000 acres in the midwest from his father. It was in the heart of America's grain belt, and the black gold, spoken of by the Dutch and Irish immigrants who cut the forests, was the soil.

Until he went to college, Kenneth had risen every day at 5:30 A.M. to help with the chores. On a large farm like theirs, most of the manual labor was to keep the machinery going, but Kenneth's father was from the old school and believed a farm boy needed to know the soil so Kenneth always had a five-acre tract of his own to farm. He used the old '46 Ford tractor—still in use after thirty years. Kenneth loved the farm and had only one desire in life: to become a farmer like his father before him.

Kenneth's father realized that the operation of a large farm required a lot more information than in previous generations, so he sent Kenneth off to the state agricultural college where he learned the latest planting techniques, scientific animal husbandry, how to utilize computers, and, most important, agrarian economics.

"Today's modern farmer learns how to use his assets wisely," the professors told their students. "Equity is idle capital and is as wasteful to farming as weak seed."

The school offered courses in how to use the latest government farm support programs to get better yield (monetarily) from the modern farm. Kenneth learned that the federal government would not only lend farmers money at subsidized interest rates, but would actually pay them not to grow certain crops. By rotating the land into the soil bank program, a farmer could revitalize the soil while getting paid by the government to do so.

"The day of the independent farmer is over," Kenneth heard over and over again. Adapt or fail—that was the byword in modern agricultural schools.

Kenneth graduated from college and worked with his father for nearly ten years, during which time he attempted with no success to get his father to apply for the farm subsidy program.

His father's response was, "I have never taken welfare, and I don't intend to start now. You never get something for nothing," he cautioned Kenneth. "One day you'll run the farm, and you would do well to remember that."

Unfortunately, "Common Sense 101" was not a required course in college, and Kenneth was chafing at the bit to apply what he had been taught. He respected his father but felt he was too old-fashioned. Fresh in his mind was the message his professors had implanted: "adapt or fail."

Eventually Kenneth could not stand to wait any longer. He told his father that he wanted to start a farm of his own and prove what he could do by using modern methodology. Kenneth's father, nearly seventy, decided that it was time to retire and turned the operation over to him.

Kenneth immediately applied to the soil bank program and committed nearly three hundred acres to the government's "don't grow food" program so generously provided by the American taxpayers. In return he received a subsidy of nearly $50,000 a year not to grow something he wasn't planning to grow anyway.

Using the crop subsidy, he then applied to the Farm Loan Administration for money to expand his operation. With the subsequent loans he modernized his equipment, and he used the tax credits to shelter virtually all the income from the farm bank subsidy. With virtually no effort he increased the farm's income by $50,000 a year, tax free (less the interest on the loan of course). The farm loan was a 4 percent expense, of which approximately half was returned in taxes. So he netted a 2 percent loan. Not a bad deal by any standard.

> ## *Kenneth was a microcosm of the Keynesian economic theory: The government can decide best how the country's resources should be used.*

As other farms became available, Kenneth made additional loans against the increasing equity in his farm to purchase them. Although the debt continued to grow, the equity in the land grew even faster. Bankers were anxious to make Kenneth any loans he wanted; he was the showcase of the Federal Farm Loan credit system.

Twice in the next five years Kenneth was named "Farmer of the Year" by national magazines. He was known as an astute young farmer who epitomized the best the "system" had to offer. Even Kenneth's father had to admit that the farm was running better and making more profit than ever before. What he didn't know, of course, was that the debt was over $2 million by the end of the fifth year. Prospects were great, and the government was planning bigger and better subsidy programs at the behest of the politicians from the farm belt.

Kenneth's farm covered more than 10,000 acres and, other than a few small tracts that had not yet become available, was virtually contiguous, making his farm the largest in the district. At age thirty-five, Kenneth was well on his way to becoming the wealthiest farmer in his entire state. He knew all the politicians by name, and they often used him as their feature attraction when asking for more subsidies from Washington. Kenneth was a microcosm of the Keynesian economic theory: The *govern-*

ment can decide best how the country's resources should be used.

Then suddenly inflation struck and loans that had been running at 8 percent escalated to 12 and later to 20 percent. The low-interest loans Kenneth had originally received had been supplanted by variable-rate, high-interest loans to a large degree.

But the added costs didn't particularly worry Kenneth. Even at the higher interest rates, he had the cash flow to survive until the economy turned around again. Besides, he knew he could always sell a part of the farm, if absolutely necessary. The federal subsidies had made his land very valuable.

What Kenneth didn't know was that the federal government was having trouble with its own budget, and one of the areas to be reduced was farm subsidies. When Ronald Reagan came into office, he brought with him some temporary, but very harsh, controls on federal spending. Within a few months, the mood in Washington had shifted from praising the farmers who fell into line with the subsidy program to accusing them of being greedy money grubbers who were getting rich at the expense of the poor.

---

*The private sector debt
is growing just as wildly
as the public sector debt.*

Suddenly Kenneth found himself on the outside looking in, as far as Washington was concerned. The farm subsidy program was altered to prohibit many of the big farms from participating. Congressional investigations were discussed to see which politicians had benefited by endorsing the big farmers.

Without warning, farm land plummeted in value as buyers realized the free ride was coming to an end. Kenneth's bankers began demanding that he reduce some of his debt. To do so required that he put a portion of his land up for sale. As soon as that word got out, land prices in his area plummeted even further.

The bankers, now concerned about Kenneth's solvency, demanded payment in full. When he couldn't comply, they forced a liquidation. In less than six years, Kenneth had gone from inheriting a thousand-acre, debt-free farm to being wiped out.

When the final parcel of land was auctioned off, Kenneth had lost a three-generation farm, all the equipment, his parents' home, and was left owing nearly $2 million to the Farm Credit Association and several banks.

It's interesting to note that the land wasn't changed, and people still needed food. But Kenneth could no longer operate any portion of the farm profitably. He didn't just lose what he had increased; he lost everything! Proverbs 23:4-5 speaks to this principle when it says, "Do not weary yourself to gain riches, cease from your consideration of it. When you set your eyes on it, it is gone. For wealth certainly makes itself wings, like an eagle that flies toward the heavens."

THE ERROR

At first glance anyone with common sense would say, "He overextended, and he should have known better." If that's true (and it is), what about the rest of the country? Kenneth was not doing anything that the majority of American businessmen and women are not doing right this minute. The private sector debt is growing just as wildly as the public sector debt. The only difference is that the government's debt is published for all to see. The private sector's debt is spread out over thousands of individuals and businesses, so it looks less imposing.

The debt picture in America today is alarming. Not only is the size unmanageable but, as noted previously, much of the interest paid is leaving the country. The small debtors borrow from the banks (and others). The banks place a large portion of their earnings in government securities (otherwise known as debt). The government in turn pays out a huge chunk of this in interest to foreign lenders, who then use their profits to reinvest in American businesses. A whole nation is literally selling its birthright, as Esau did for the proverbial "bowl of soup."

A look at America's debt structure today should be enough to get the attention of any doubters.

PERSONAL DEBT

Prior to the 1920s, Americans were characterized as frugal, self-reliant people who had a strong faith in God. Debt was certainly not unknown, but it would have been unusual for the average American to borrow for anything other than the purchase of a home, and even that loan was for no more than seven years or less.

It is not by chance that most private debt was limited to a payout of seven years or less. The plan for all lending had been adopted from the Bible and, as such, the duration of loans was patterned after the year of remission described in Deuteronomy 15:1-2: "At the end of every seven years you shall grant a remission of debts. And this is the manner of remission: every creditor shall release what he has loaned to his neighbor; he shall not exact it of his neighbor and his brother, because the Lord's remission has been proclaimed."

As I said earlier, the real trend in consumer debt began after World War II, with the return of millions of GIs needing homes, cars, and jobs. Americans had a great deal of disposable income and were able to handle debt on long-term purchases such as homes. A look at the average family's disposable income in 1960 gives a clear picture of where the country was financially.

By the early seventies the great credit card binge was under way.

The average income was approximately $6,700 per year. Out of that income, the average family paid 8 percent in direct taxes (including Social Security). Their home costs amounted to 22 percent of net income. The average home sold for just over $8,000, was about 1,000 square feet, carried a twenty-one-year loan at 4.5 percent, and was soon to yield some huge appreciation.

A new car in 1960 sold for approximately $2,100 and could be financed for as long as eighteen months, provided the buyer put down at least 25 percent.

Beyond that, the average family carried no debt except, occasionally, some credit for appliances financed by one of the national retailers such as Sears or J. C. Penney.

It was actually this seemingly insignificant area of retail credit that would spark the consumer credit binge in America. By the mid-sixties, most of the major retailers were offering credit for purchases. Surprisingly consumers accepted the idea of retail credit, even though the interest rates were significantly higher than that of commercial lenders, like banks. The key factor was that the retailers made credit available to many families (especially young couples) who could not qualify for bank loans.

In the forties, fifties, and early sixties, bankers were noted for their conservative approach to lending. Basically, they wouldn't lend for consumables and wouldn't lend to people who should not have had credit. In other words, you had to earn the right to receive credit.

I can recall applying for my first home loan in 1962, while working at Cape Canaveral in Florida. Although I had a good job and could well afford the payments of $86 per month on a three-bedroom home that sold for $8,200 (wouldn't we like to see that again?), because I had no credit history the bank turned me down. Only later, after we had saved an additional $1,000, were we able to qualify for a loan.

Credit cards were a rarity at that time, with the exception of specialty cards such as American Express. In 1963 I applied for a credit card (although I didn't particularly need it), but I was turned down because American Express required at least a $10,000 per year income to qualify for one of their cards.

I'm sure you get the picture: Americans had adjusted to home mortgages, car loans, and some consumer financing for major appliances, but the credit boom was still to come.

By the mid-sixties financial reports from the big retailers began to reflect huge profits from the consumer credit they were issuing. Suddenly the rush was on to tap into that lucrative market. Stores like Sears were making as much on financing as they were making on the merchandise, and with a whole lot less effort. Remarkably the defaults by consumers had proved to be nominal by banking standards. Americans were prone to protect their reputations and pay their bills. By the early seventies the great credit card binge was under way.

In the housing area more and more home buyers entered the market created by long-term mortgages. Soon the law of supply and demand began to kick in. The law (rule really) of supply and demand is simple: With an abundant supply of any product and a shortage of available buyers, prices will remain constant or fall; with a shortage of any product and an abundance of buyers, prices will rise.

In this case, the availability of long-term financing for housing opened up the product (homes) to many additional buyers. Consequently they bid the price of homes up, and the housing boom was under way.

As prices escalated, the number of home buyers who could qualify began to decline. Faced with a declining demand, the lending institutions simply lengthened the terms of the mortgages, thus qualifying more buyers. This spiral took the average mortgage period from twelve years to thirty years in just one decade. At the same time, the average home escalated in price from $8,600 to $26,000.

Less than 2 percent of all Americans own their homes debt-free.

This sparked a real estate boom that was to continue for the next twenty-five years. Americans began to view their homes not only as dwelling places but also as good investments.

Any supply and demand spiral can only grow until the price of the product (homes in this case) is beyond what the average consumer can afford, even with the long-term financing. Then prices will begin to fall again. The reason this process was delayed in the case of residential housing was not just long-term financing but also because potential buyers took on dual incomes (husband and wife) to qualify; they stretched their housing budget from 22 percent in 1960 to more than 40 percent in 1990 and took on some "creative" mortgages to expand their buying range.

The most recent "creative" mortgage plan is the adoption of a ninety-year payment schedule. Effectively Americans have mortgaged their futures to buy the homes they have come to expect. Even the recent trend back to smaller, simpler homes has not brought the average home within the income range of the average family. The current median income per family is $36,000 (1991). Based on this income, an average home should sell for approximately $72,000. Instead, it sells for just under $108,000. Those who buy at these prices, and many do, find themselves in constant financial difficulties.

> ## One problem with so much consumer indebtedness is that the average wage earner is also the government's primary provider.

In 1980 it was estimated that Americans had usable equity of about $180 billion in their homes, relative to disposable incomes (the ability to make payments on the loans). As a result of the 1086 Tax Reform Act, which allows deductions only for home related loans, that usable equity has now dropped to an estimated $100 billion. As Americans borrowed against the equity in their homes, they used a larger portion of their disposable incomes. As a recent study by the President's Council on the Family showed, if the real value of homes was accurately reflected (what a qualified buyer is willing and able to pay) Americans would have a negative equity (usable for collateral) in their homes. With only 2 percent of Americans owning their homes without a debt, and the average length of a mortgage at twenty-two years remaining, that does not bode well for our banking system.

American banks now hold nearly $2 trillion in first mortgages as collateral for what are considered the most stable loans in their portfolios. In addition, they hold nearly $80 billion in home equity loans above the first mortgages. These also are considered some of the "best" loans. Clearly American home owners have transferred the wealth stored in their homes to the lenders. In this case, it leaves both in jeopardy. Given the wrong set of economic circumstances, the homeowners will default, leaving the banks with huge inventories of homes they can't sell.

CONSUMER DEBT

The rise in consumer debt over the last twenty years has been nothing less than phenomenal—from approximately $131 billion in 1970 to more than $794 billion in 1990! And the alarming fact about consumer debt is that it is available to virtually anyone and usually carries an annual finance charge of 18 percent and higher.

Literally, Americans are working for the "company store" again. They labor at their jobs to pay the usurious interest they have come to accept as "normal." The increase in personal bankruptcies has grown at an alarming pace. In 1970 the total of personal bankruptcies was under 100,000. In 1980 it was 259,160, but by 1985 bankruptcies had risen to 312,000. In 1990 there were 685,439, and although official statistics are not available for 1991, the unofficial estimate is 900,000 plus. At the rate personal bankruptcies grew during the last decade, it is estimated they will reach four million by the year 2000—and that's with no major economic crisis. This is not a problem. It is a symptom of a society awash in "easy money," which is what credit seems to be today. Eventually the majority of households will reach the stage where they cannot repay what they owe, nor will they be able to borrow more. At that point, the economy must stop while the debt is either repudiated (by a depression), devalued (by hyperinflation), or repaid (unthinkable).

A CATCH 22

One problem with so much consumer indebtedness is that the average wage earner is also the government's primary provider. As I said previously, in spite of all the rhetoric you hear from the liberal side of the media and from the Congress, it is not the wealthy who can carry the tax burden in America (or any other country). The truth is, there just simply are not enough of them.

At this point, I would like to stop and offer an observation that is critical to our economy's long-term survival.

The system of economics by which our wealth was developed is called "capitalism." Capitalism means that private individuals with a surplus of capital are willing to risk it to make more capital. That process inevitably makes some of them wealthy. But also in the process others are employed, and some of them save enough to invest and become "capitalists."

There is nothing inherently bad or evil about this system, as the media often represents. It is this capitalistic system that has allowed us the ability to support other poorer countries, defend our freedoms, and do away with child labor.

If we now treat all the wealthy "capitalists" like criminals simply because some are criminals, we will lose our economic base and we will sink to the level of "socialist" countries such as Russia, China, Yugoslavia, Poland, Hungary, and so on.

Borrowed capital became the primary means of starting new businesses in the late sixties and seventies.

The Bible does not teach against the accumulation of wealth as some apparently believe. It teaches against greed, ego, and a disregard for the needs of others. Anyone who thinks that the lack of wealth is a cure for these sins has only to visit any major inner city in America today.

The vast majority of people with a surplus of money did not steal it or cheat someone else to get it. They made it doing what they are best at. Anyone who now believes the government can do a better job of managing that money by stripping it from those who have it needs to look at the evidence to the contrary. The government does not invest; it consumes. Politicians who use the system to their advantage would be quite willing to consume the nation's "seed corn" if it would help them get re-elected. Our single hope of economic recovery (outside of divine intervention) resides in the American entrepreneur's ability to see a need and fill it. Without the available capital, that is not possible. I am not touting the wealthy because I am one, because I am not; but I do know that America must have investment capital to survive, and the poor just don't have it.

It is the average income wage earner to whom the government will always turn when there is a need for more tax money. The quickest and least painful way (for the politicians) to raise money to keep the government operating is to create some new "revenue enhancements." Since tax increases are politically unpopular, the common method used is to initiate a tax bill designed to "soak the rich" and drop in a few revenue enhancers, such as eliminating the interest deduction for mortgages or the write-offs for contributions. There are several other possibilities, but these two will generate nearly $100 billion a year in new taxes by themselves. The unfortunate by-product of this action is to reduce the average consumer's level of spending. Therein lies the "Catch 22."

The increased tax revenues are offset by decreased spending. The decreased spending means fewer sales, which means fewer jobs, which means less revenue. . . .

BUSINESS DEBT

The trend in business debt is not as startling as that of the consumers, but it is equally as disastrous. As of 1990, American businesses were paying out 7.7 percent of their gross incomes in interest alone—compared to 3.8 percent in 1970. Total business debt rose from $62 billion in 1970 to just over $700 billion in 1990. Much of this is debt on nonproductive capital, such as the junk bonds used for leveraged buy-outs during the eighties. Other companies that were not engaged in leveraged buy-outs took on considerable debt during this time in an effort to make their businesses less enticing to a buy-out. These were the so-called "poison pills" swallowed by so many companies. The leveraged buy-outs have ceased, but many of the poison pills are still around.

A look at American business prior to the sixties shows that the majority of businesses were started and expanded by selling equity. Basically this meant selling stock in the company and giving up a portion of the equity. Two things happened in the sixties and seventies that changed the funding strategies of most businesses from equity to debt.

First, credit became readily available at competitive rates. In fact, the cost of renting the money was considerably less than the profits that could be made by using the money in the business. There is no question that it made economic sense to borrow money at 6 percent and invest it in a business that could yield 10 to 12 percent a year on the money. Borrowed capital became the primary means of starting new businesses in the late sixties and seventies. As business loans became more commonplace, companies even shifted to debt funding for expansion as well as for acquisition. By the mid-seventies debt was the acceptable means of starting and operating a business.

The second change was that the cost of issuing stock became prohibitively expensive for many small companies. The complexities of the securities laws and the risks in the stock market forced most start-up operations to rely totally on debt funding.

Limited partnerships were an attempt by the securities groups to provide an alternative means of selling equity. Unfortunately the abuses by fast-talking promoters virtually killed this avenue for equity funding in the eighties. Eventually the abuse of tax laws in limited partnerships caused the demise of that system.

The vast majority of equity in American companies is still found in stocks traded on the two major exchanges. But the largest portions of these stocks are sold investor to investor. Their sales do not particularly help the parent company, except to the extent that stockholders' equity goes up. For a company to profit from the sale of its stock there must be either a new issue offered for sale or existing treasury stock sold. Most transactions do virtually nothing to benefit the company's daily operations except that it makes loans easier to acquire, based on equity values.

The debt burden of most businesses in America today is so great that virtually any slowdown in economic activity can place them in jeopardy. This was clearly demonstrated in the early stages of the 1990 recession when many major department store chains went under due to poor Christmas sales. These retailers had taken on so much debt that even a single slow season wiped them out. Some were chains that had been in operation for five decades or more, like the Federated Department Stores.

Certainly competition from mass marketers, such as Wal-Mart and K-Mart, had affected these retailers to some extent. But generally they were not direct competitors in the same market share. It was excessive debt that did them in; and it is excessive debt that will do in a great many more businesses in any prolonged downturn. Unfortunately this presents a dilemma to the politicians in a government-controlled economy like ours: How can we collect all the taxes possible without killing off the businesses that employ the people who pay the taxes? I believe the answer to that question is the key to the coming economic earthquake. . . .

The time is approaching when the government can no longer fund its overspending without destroying the business base of America. When that time comes, there will be few options available other than the printing of more money. Every nation that has gone this route has sparked hyperinflation that eventually wiped out the middle class.

9
Government Debt

Imagine this scenario if you will: A family of four making $3,000 a month is spending $4,000 a month and has been doing so for more than five years. Their total assets consist of a home and two cars—all mortgaged for more than their resale value. Their total debt to date is $150,000 in unsecured liabilities, plus an additional $100,000 they have borrowed from their retirement account, which must be repaid with interest in the next twenty years. And one last item: They borrowed their parents' life savings to help pay the interest on their debt and now are obligated to support them, in addition to their own current spending.

Let's assume this couple has come to you for advice about what they should do at this point. How would you counsel them?

Having counseled many couples in the past, I can tell you the options:

1. They can try to generate more income, but essentially this husband is working at his capacity, so the most he can hope to get is a part-time job that will generate another couple of hundred a month.

2. They can file for bankruptcy protection and just not pay most of their creditors. Of course this will destroy their reputation and their credit rating for the indefinite future. In addition, it won't help the repayment of their retirement account or the money they have borrowed from their parents.

3. They can find someone who will lend them the money to consolidate all their debts. But, since the total debt is still beyond their ability to pay even if they consolidate, they will need enough extra to make the monthly payments for the next several years, at which time they are hoping that something miraculous will happen to pay off the entire debt.

Actually, now you find out that they have not come to you for advice but for a consolidation loan, since you seem to be doing pretty well yourself.

The government has an income of approximately $1.4 trillion a year. It is spending approximately $1.8 trillion a year.

Logically, I hope you would say, "It seems to me that you need to get realistic and face the facts: You simply spend too much for your income. Sell whatever you can, pay down the debt, cut back your spending, and start paying back what you owe. More money won't help at this point."

Good advice, I would say. Only the couple in this case is our government. The numbers used are smaller than the government's total income and debt, but the ratios are correct.

The government has an income of approximately $1.4 trillion a year. It is spending approximately $1.8 trillion a year.

The total "on budget" debt of the government is $3.8 trillion as of late 1991; and the "off-budget" debt, which includes unfunded retirement liabilities, is another $2.5 trillion.

The money the government has borrowed from its "parents" is the Social Security Trust Funds taken from millions of honest Americans who believe they are contributing to their own retirement accounts.

We are in a mess that is getting messier every day, and there appears to be no interest in trying to resolve the problems. The only concern shown by most politicians is how to fund the deficits without changing the system or their own spending habits, which include incomes four times higher than the average workers they represent and a very generous retirement plan.

HOW IMPORTANT IS THE DEBT?

I have to confess that the naïveté of some of our elected officials astounds me. I used to think they suffered from ignorance, but the facts are evident for all to see: The national debt is undermining the very freedoms we cherish.

In the last several years a new "theory" has been developed in Washington that the national debt really doesn't matter since it is a smaller ratio of the country's gross national product (GNP) than it was thirty years ago. That is not true.

In 1980 the GNP was $2.7 trillion and the total debt was $914 billion—a ratio of 2.95 to 1. In 1990 the GNP was $5.4 trillion and the total debt was $3.8 trillion—a ratio of 1.42 to 1. Add to that figure the off-budget debt, and you get a better picture of the total. With a real national debt in excess of $6 trillion, the total debt is actually greater than the GNP. But even if it were not, the argument still makes no sense. The very fact that so much debt has been used in the economy inflates the GNP. For example: If housing contributes $1 trillion to the GNP, how much of that is inflation, created by excessive long-term financing?

To determine this, just assume that today a law was passed making all mortgages illegal so that no home could be sold with a mortgage. Therefore, if you wanted to sell your home, you would have to find a cash buyer.

Under these circumstances what would a $100,000 home (present value) sell for across the country? Not $100,000—that's for sure. On a cash-only basis, it would probably sell for about $20,000 (the supply and demand rule). We can logically assume that everything above that amount has been added through debt-funded inflation. The national debt has added to the GNP by virtue of inflation. If adjusted for inflation since 1980, the nation's GNP is actually $4.3 trillion.

But let's use this argument: Sure, the GNP is calculated in inflated dollars, but so is the debt itself. The next issue: How much of the government's income does it take to make the payments now, as compared to even ten years ago?

In 1980 it took approximately 12 percent of the government's income to service its debt. To date, it requires approximately 18 percent (40 percent of all personal income taxes).

In 1980 the per capita indebtedness was approximately $4,000. Average median income (per family) was $18,700—a ratio of 21 percent of annual income.

By 1990 the average indebtedness was approximately $15,000 per capita, with an average annual income of $30,000—a ratio of 50 percent of annual income! I would like someone to explain how the national debt doesn't really matter today!

FIGURES DON'T LIE

As the old cliche goes: "Figures don't lie, but liars can figure." The following chart clearly shows the ever-widening gap between federal revenues and federal spending.

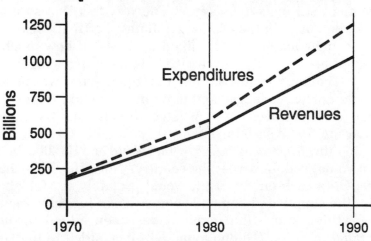

Expenditures vs. Revenues

Source: U.S. Department of the Treasury

The growth of the national debt has been alarming, but the process by which it is allowed to grow is equally alarming.

The president and the Congress are required by law to submit a budget each year that demonstrates all spending is within the government's income. Because of past abuses of the "system," a new law was passed in 1985 requiring the government not only to live within its income but also to balance the federal budget in six years and begin repaying some of the existing debt. This law, the Gramm-Rudman Act, was to be the guiding force behind fiscal responsibilities. But before looking at the new law, it is enlightening to look at the old law (which still exists).

Each year the White House sends Congress its estimates of income and expenditures. The Congress is then required to send to the president a budget demonstrating that income and outgo match. Since this is obviously not the case, there has to be some mechanism by which deficit spending is approved. Debt funding is accomplished by the Congress appropriating a "temporary" budget extension, which allows the deficit to be funded through loans from the public.

This provision was intended to be a "crisis" exception so the country could borrow on a temporary basis to continue operations on an emergency basis. It was presumed that our leaders would never be foolish enough to borrow during good economic times, so no definitive limitations were included. Consequently the Congress has been exercising this exception every year since 1940, with only two years of balanced budgets since the end of World War II; so the exception became the rule in Congress.

When the budget and national debt began to swell in the seventies, some conservative taxpayers began a "balance the budget" movement to require the government to live within its means. There was even talk of a constitutional amendment to force a balanced budget on the politicians, since they didn't seem willing to do so voluntarily.

When Ronald Reagan came into the presidency, some members of Congress began to feel the momentum building toward such an amendment. There was even talk of opening another constitutional convention to correct some other liberal interpretations of the constitution. Suddenly the Congress was open to a new law requiring a balanced budget. Thus, they approved the Gramm-Rudman Act—first in 1985, and when that didn't work, they tried again in 1987. The Gramm-Rudman laws set down specific yearly guidelines for reducing the budget deficits according to the following chart.

Budget Deficit

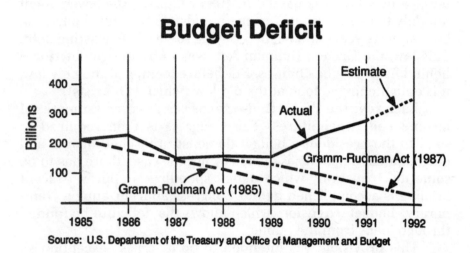

Source: U.S. Department of the Treasury and Office of Management and Budget

As you can see, the original law required that the federal budget be balanced by the year 1991. In addition, overruns in excess of the prescribed amounts initiated automatic spending cuts. Unfortunately, both laws left some "loop-holes" and depended too much on the *integrity* of those in charge of our government—something that is sorely missing today. As you can see from the comparison, the legal annual deficit and the actual deficits grow further apart each year.

The Congress and the president have simply found "creative" ways around the law. One method is to siphon the funds out of the Social Security Trust account and use them to help reduce the deficits. As I said previously, since the theft is considered an internal transfer of assets, it is not reflected as a debt (very creative, huh?).

Another technique is to transfer budget overruns into the next fiscal year. You might logically think that would create an even greater problem the next year. Not so! All you have to do is transfer that amount (and more) into the next year (now that's also very creative).

The third method is even more creative. Since the budget and its deficits are calculated on projected income, it is a simple process to calculate more income than is realistic during the budget process. Then when the overruns are greater than anticipated, the budget managers simply say, "Oops," and ask for a special dispensation for that error.

The last creative technique used in the budgeting process is simply to ignore the law altogether by shifting more spending "off budget." If you or I did that, it would be punishable by fines and imprisonment; but for our elected "leaders," it is "business as usual." In the adoption of the "balanced budget" law, the Congress excluded the majority of spending from the budget process. Thus, areas such as welfare, Medicare, Social Security, federal retirement, and the like are exempt from the mandatory reductions. To balance the budget based on actual income and expenses would require the virtual elimination of other "flexible" areas of spending, such as defense. The exclusions make a balanced budget virtually impossible.

I'm sure you get the picture by now. The net effect is to continue the budget overruns irrespective of the law. After all, the elected leaders of our nation exempt themselves from every other law they require of the voters. Why not exempt themselves from the laws passed to control their actions?

RUNAWAY DEBT

When the Grace Commission was authorized by President Reagan in 1983, it was a privately funded, nonpartisan group, directed to find ways to cut government waste, which they did. But as a by-product, they began to look into the huge budget deficits and resultant debt being accumulated by the government. As Harry Figgie, a member of the commission, said, "It wasn't just alarming. It was frightening." Of course, that was before the Gramm-Rudman Act required the budget to be balanced by 1991.

At the time of the Commission's report in 1984, they estimated the total federal debt might reach $3 trillion by the year 2000. As we saw earlier, it exceeded that level in 1991.

Every time the taxpayers
give the Congress $1.00 extra,
they spend $1.68.

All realistic estimates now place the potential debt at $13 to $20 trillion by the year 2000. That may sound distant to those of us who have lived most of our lives in the twentieth century, but it is less than ten years away.

The following chart demonstrates what the accumulated deficit will look like in just a few years. I included this chart again because it is critical to understand that the debt is going to destroy our economy if it is not brought under control quickly.

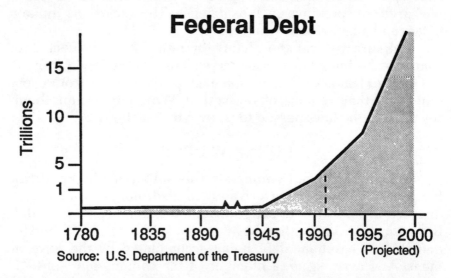

Federal Debt

Source: U.S. Department of the Treasury   (Projected)

Mr. Figgie relates a story that typifies what happens in the budgeting process in Washington. He said that in 1986 the Congress adopted $152 billion of the $424 billion in savings identified by the Grace Commission. At the same time, because of the urgent concern about the skyrocketing debt, the Congress voted for a $50 billion tax increase (the 1986 Tax "Reform" Act).

As a result of these two changes, which amounted to a $38 billion decrease in spending for five consecutive years and a $50 billion increase in revenues, the annual deficit, which was $128 billion at that time, should have been $40 billion by 1991 ($128 minus $38 = $90 minus $50 = $40). Instead, the "on-budget" annual deficit is closer to $258 billion. That does not include the S&L deficits, which are considered "off budget."

As Mr. Figgie points out, every time the taxpayers give the Congress $1.00 extra, it spends $1.68.

This discussion about the federal debt is an attempt to bring you up to date on what's *really* happening with the deficit in Washington. Not only is it out of control, there appears to be no rational voice in the capitol trying to straighten out the mess. I can't emphasize too strongly that the federal debt (as well as the private sector debt) can and will destroy our economy. Americans who have worked hard all their lives will see their life savings consumed by runaway inflation. Remember that the politicians who tell you that the debt is irrelevant are the same ones who said the following: More money will eliminate poverty; taxes will never be more than 2 percent; pornography is a personal issue; and sex education will solve teen pregnancies. With that kind of a track record, I doubt that their insight about this issue is any better.

The one thing you can be sure of is that when the deficits begin to go ballistic and rob businesses of the capital they need to operate, and when huge chunks of American industry are sold off to foreign investors to secure needed operating capital, the Congress will hold investigations to determine why this was allowed to happen.

At the current rate of growth, the federal deficits will feed approximately $7 trillion dollars of additional debt into the economy between 1992 and the year 2000. There never has been anything approaching this level of debt funding in the history of mankind in so short a period of time, even on a percentage basis. The effects of this will be felt throughout the U.S. and ultimately the world's economies. It is estimated that, at most, approximately $3 to $5 trillion is available from all sources to fund this deficit. That leaves only two logical conclusions: Either the government will take the necessary steps to control the budget and reduce the deficits drastically, or they will resort to monetizing (creating) the debt by printing massive amounts of new currency.

I don't know what your analysis is but, based on observation, I find it hard to believe our government leaders have either the inclination or the will to cut their spending sufficiently.

---

*Does anyone realistically believe
that politicians are going to
make the kinds of choices
necessary to balance the budget?*

Allow me to outline what kinds of cuts would be necessary to bring the budget into balance over the next five years. This does not deal with reducing the national debt—only the annual deficits that are adding to it presently.

1. All federal payrolls would need to be reduced by approximately 40 percent. This would require the dismissal of 1.3 million employees, saving approximately $40 billion annually.

2. Welfare would need to be reduced by 25 percent, saving $46.5 billion annually.

3. Defense spending would need to be reduced by 25 percent, saving $10 billion annually. (This would require the closure of 3,000 obsolete military installations all across the country, resulting in the additional loss of 300,000 jobs in civilian-related businesses.) It would also necessitate recalling at least one-half of all active U.S. military personnel stationed outside the United States.

4. Entitlement programs, such as student loans, farm support, education grants, and the myriad of other government-subsidized programs would need to be cut across the board by at least 25 percent, saving $60 billion.

As you can see, even with these cuts the budget has been reduced by only $146.5 billion a year. We would need to make another round of cuts to trim out the additional $200 billion in actual overspending, if the government could not shift any spending to the off-budget category.

My obvious question is: Does anyone realistically believe that politicians are going to make the kinds of choices necessary to balance the budget? And would the average American be willing to make the sacrifices necessary to allow such cuts, even if the politicians wanted to do so?

Unfortunately this is not the end of the debt spiral; it is barely the beginning unless an immediate attitude adjustment is made in our country. There are some future trends that can make the present level of spending look like the "good ol' days."

We have some pending problems that need resolution, and unfortunately the common attitude is that throwing money at problems will make them go away. One might think we should know better, based on our "success" record to date.

Logic and common sense seem to play small parts in our present society, as confirmed by the following facts:

• We get soft on prosecuting criminals and then wonder why crime increases.

• We legalize abortion and then wonder why there are fewer kids to fill the schools.

• We protect child pornography as free speech and then wonder why so many kids are abducted and murdered.

• We take discipline out of the classrooms and wonder why kids don't learn as well.

• We entice young couples to get into debt and then wonder why the divorce rate is so high.

The list could go on and on. The answer is found in God's Word. All of these things are but *symptoms*. The real problem is that we have removed God from the decision-making process in America today. When any nation does this, evil will prosper. This is not the fault of the politicians; they are responding to the wishes of the most vocal groups. It is that the unprincipled people around us seem to be more committed to their agenda than the true "moral majority" are to theirs. This conforms with what the Lord said in Luke 16:8: "And his master praised the unrighteous steward because he had acted shrewdly; for the sons of this age are more shrewd in relation to their own kind than the sons of light."

What I have tried to do thus far is bring you up-to-date on what has happened in the economy. Even if we could freeze the spending right where it is, the debt would eventually become unmanageable, simply because of the accumulating interest. The following graph shows the annual interest "payments" just since 1980. Interest "payments" is a misnomer. The interest is not actually being paid. It is being borrowed and added to the debt. So, in reality, we are paying interest on the interest from previous years.

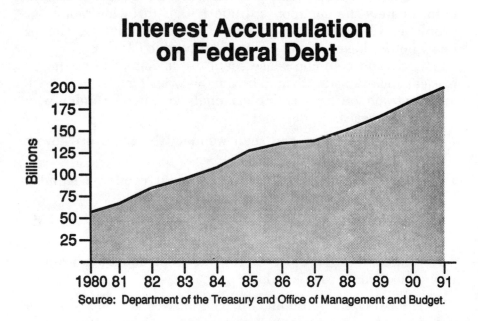

Interest Accumulation on Federal Debt

Source: Department of the Treasury and Office of Management and Budget.

Using an annualized interest rate of 8 percent and a budget deficit growing at the rate of $250 billion a year, the next chart projects the interest payments on the debt through the end of this decade.

This graph is a projection of the interest payments assuming no increase in spending. It also does not include the $400 billion or so necessary for the S&L bailout.

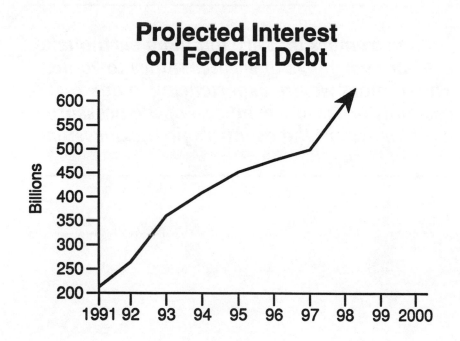

Projected Interest on Federal Debt

The tremors that are felt in an earthquake zone are warnings of greater things to come. The tremors we are experiencing in our economy are also warnings—of the pressures building within the country's financial system.

10
Tremors

In most earthquake-prone areas, small tremors are a fact of life. I can remember the first time I felt a tremor. I was attending a meeting in southern California, and suddenly the room vibrated like an off-balance washing machine (the best analogy I could think of back then). It lasted less than a second; then it was gone.

Those of us who had never experienced tremors before were wide-eyed. But the native Californians never even put their coffee cups down. I can remember thinking, *These people are too blasé. Those rumblings are a warning of greater things to come.*

Earth tremors are an indication of unstable geological forces. In a way, they are good because they relieve some of the stresses building up. But the inhabitants must never forget that they are also warnings not to build fragile homes in a fault area.

As the tremors build in intensity, the warnings should be attended carefully. In an actual earthquake, not much can be done except to follow emergency procedures. But, in the case of an economic earthquake, changes could be made to relieve the stresses, but only if enough people are aware and *demand* action.

The following are presented as tremors signaling the excessive buildup of economic stress.

TREMOR NUMBER 1:
THE SAVINGS AND LOAN COLLAPSE

Tremors often rumble past us, giving warnings of greater catastrophes to come if no changes are made. The Savings and Loan debacle is just one of these. The total effect on the economy has yet to be felt. Essentially it is twofold: the immediate effect is a direct cost to the taxpayers of some $400 billion to cover the losses suffered by insured depositors. Some of this cost will eventually be recovered by selling off the assets held by the Resolution Trust Corporation (RTC).

A look into the S&L industry collapse is a glimpse at a typical government-enhanced debacle. During the eighties the government encouraged the S&Ls to loosen their loan standards to stimulate economic growth, particularly in the construction industry. At the same time, the 1982 tax changes gave huge tax benefits to private investors to encourage them to risk their money in new real estate ventures. The combination of these two incentives stimulated an unprecedented commercial real estate boom throughout most of the eighties.

Without question, there were some crooks and thieves in the S&L business, attracted by the looser regulations and profits to be made. But the majority of the S&Ls were run by honest business people who were responding to the direction provided from Washington. Although few senators and congressmen will admit to endorsing the plan now, they certainly did when their constituents were prospering from it during the Reagan administration.

The Tax Reform Act, passed in 1986, brought with it sweeping tax changes designed to "soak the rich." A part of the new law changed the rules for real estate tax incentives—retroactively. In other words, the government reneged on the agreement that it had made with investors, which allowed them to use real estate tax shelters to offset some of their ordinary income. As a result, investors pulled out of the real estate development business—*en masse*. Existing partnerships that required additional annual payments saw investors default rather than put any more money into the projects.

Consequently, many commercial projects became insolvent, and along with them some of the S&Ls that had partially or fully backed the projects. There is no doubt that some of the previous tax laws were ill-conceived and did little more than promote overbuilding. But a deal is a deal, and when the government reneges on a contract it has made, the result is a further eroding of public trust. I knew of several politicians who spoke out against the retroactive application of the new tax changes. Their comments fell on deaf ears in the Congress and White House as politicians feared being aligned with the rich against the poor.

During the same period in which the tax laws were changed, the oil industry was suffering a major downturn, and real estate development in the Texas and Oklahoma "oil patch" hit a depression. The drain on S&L assets actually started in Texas, where many lenders found themselves in deep trouble. The dual effects of lower oil prices and investor withdrawals plunged the S&Ls into virtual collapse.

More stringent regulations were applied in an apparent attempt to placate screaming politicians who were bent on blaming somebody else.

By 1988 it was obvious that some major S&Ls were going to fail and would require a bailout by the government (taxpayers) to save the depositors' money. This sparked an investigation by the banking commission, which found a great many other S&Ls in trouble because of bad real estate loans.

In typical government fashion, they slammed the barn door after the horses had fled and clamped very tight regulations on the S&L industry. As a result, only a few S&Ls could meet the new guidelines for liabilities versus assets (equity). The primary reason they could not was that they had been operating under the previous looser requirements "suggested" by Washington. Using the authority of the regulatory commission, the government seized weak S&Ls and attempted to merge them with larger S&Ls. To do this the larger S&Ls, assuming the liabilities of smaller institutions, were given special tax incentives as well as promises of loans from the central bank.

During the Bush administration, the tax incentives were withdrawn (again retroactively), and even more stringent regulations were applied in an apparent attempt to placate screaming politicians who were bent on blaming somebody else. As a result, even larger numbers of S&Ls could not meet the new solvency requirements.

As soon as this information reached the public, there was a predictable reaction: panic. Once the panic began, the S&L industry was doomed. As mentioned earlier, no banking system is safer than the public thinks it is, and the public was convinced that S&Ls in general were unsafe.

As the industry crashed, the government was left with huge inventories of properties, many of them only partially completed. A friend in Dallas typified what happened even to honest developers during this time.

Some of the biggest banks in America ... have been making loans that no prudent investor would ever have made with his own funds.

As a builder he had been in commercial construction for nearly twenty years, and although his business was going through some difficult times because of the problems in the oil industry, he had never missed a payment to the S&L with which he dealt. He had two major projects in the works at that time. One project had a loan commitment of $6 million from the S&L, on which he had drawn about $3 million to that point.

In 1988 the S&L that held his loans was declared insolvent according to the new criteria and was seized by the regulators. Finding no S&Ls willing to absorb the ailing thrift because of the more recent reversal of the tax credit policy, the government regulators shut it down and began to liquidate the assets, which included my friend's loans and the property collateralizing them.

They demanded immediate repayment of all outstanding loans and stopped all loan commitments from the now-defunct S&L. My friend argued with the government trustees that he had never missed a payment and had loan commitments from the S&L to finish his projects. He could have saved his breath. The government regulators were intractable. Six months later he was bankrupt, and the Resolution Trust Corporation, which manages the properties owned by defunct S&Ls, had possession of his properties.

Unfortunately, a half-finished project is not worth half of its finished value. In fact, without a source of development funds, it may well be worth a tenth of what has already been invested. His properties were auctioned off for less than a tenth of what had been spent to that point. The question that has to be asked is, was it bad investments or bad decisions that cost the taxpayers at least $2 million and my friend his business?

As you probably realize, about the only S&Ls that still exist are those that now call themselves Savings Banks. They fall under the control of the Federal Reserve System and are insured through the FDIC. Isn't it interesting that virtually all financial institutions, other than credit unions, now fall under the system mandated by the Keynesian economists?

TREMOR NUMBER 2:
THE BANKS

For several years, keen-eyed accountants have been warning that some of the biggest banks in America were in financial trouble. Banks like Chase Manhattan, New York City Bank, Chicago Bank and Trust, Bank of America, and dozens of others have been making loans that no prudent investor would ever have made with his own funds. Loans were made to Mexico, Brazil, Argentina, Yugoslavia, and Donald Trump—all of which were in trouble right from the beginning.

When an audit is done on most of the big banks in the country, it reads like a case study in "Banking 101" on what *not*

to do with other people's money. You may recall what was mentioned earlier: depositors aren't especially watchful of the loans
their banks are making, because their deposits are "protected"
by a national insurance plan—the FDIC.

According to a 1990 audit done on the nation's banks, there
are some 435 banks that are insolvent by *any* accounting standards. Among these are twenty of the largest banks, representing nearly $2 trillion in depositors' funds. Each dollar on deposit
is a potential debt for the government if a bank fails. The FDIC
is obligated to repay all depositors up to $100,000 per account.

---

*The profit margins in the
insurance industry have declined
as the companies have had to
get more competitive.*

In fact, so far the FDIC has covered *all* deposits, regardless
of the amount, in the large banks that have failed, such as The
Republic Bank of Dallas, Chicago's Continental Illinois Bank,
and the Bank of New England. The reason is simple: the government fears that if any depositors lose money in a large bank's
failure there could be a run on the deposits of other large banks
that would spark a major bank collapse. After all, any bank is
only as safe as you or I think it is.

Many depositors are just finding out what the bankers have
known for a decade or more: the FDIC itself is essentially broke.
At its zenith, the insurance plan only had about 5 percent reserves for the funds it insured. In the late 1980s this amount
declined to about 1.3 percent. Not to worry though. When the
final bill is due, the American taxpayers will be asked to pick up
the tab (strictly off-budget I'm sure). The logical question we
need to ask is, Where are the taxpayers going to get the money?
The banks won't fail in good times. They will fail when it is the
least opportune time, and a lot of taxpayers are going to find the
bailout very inconvenient.

TREMOR NUMBER 3:
THE INSURANCE INDUSTRY

In the first part of this book I mentioned that one of the selling features of the insurance industry is that no major insurance company failed during the Great Depression. But the economy of the nineties is not the economy of the thirties, and a great many insurance companies are in financial trouble—some because of imprudent investments in things like junk bonds but, over all, more are in trouble because of business and real estate loans they made when times were good.

According to the National Organization of Life and Health Insurance Guaranty Associations, 113 insurance companies were declared to be insolvent or impaired between 1988 and 1991, leaving millions of unpaid claims in their wake. Of course, most of these have been smaller companies. But Standard and Poor's Service, which rates all major insurance companies, is constantly downgrading the stability of some huge companies.

The collapse of the nation's eighteenth largest insurance carrier, Mutual Benefit of New Jersey, is an example of what can happen to *any* company when public confidence wanes. Mutual Benefit was downgraded by the insurance rating companies because of nonperforming commercial real estate loans. When policyholders read of Mutual Benefit's problems, they flooded the company with demands for their deposits. Within a month the company was stripped of available cash and could not meet its obligations. The New Jersey Insurance Trust assumed these policy obligations through a pooled fund set up for this purpose. Most states can handle one major company's failure before the funds are themselves exhausted.

The profit margins in the insurance industry have declined as the companies have had to get more competitive. The growth of mutual funds and the onslaught of term insurance companies have pulled cash out of many of the lower-paying, whole-life plans. Also, many life insurance companies have branched out into the health insurance field and are facing rapidly declining margins of profit (or even large losses).

For decades, the whole-life (cash value) insurance companies, which represent the backbone of the industry, benefited from decreasing mortality rates as Americans lived longer. This helped the profit margins on older policies that were priced according to earlier mortality tables. These profits faded as increased competition forced most companies to adapt to the newer mortality tables and thus lower the costs of life insurance. Now many companies are looking at potentially devastating losses from early deaths due to the AIDS epidemic.

Basically, any life insurance company makes money by investing its policyholders' deposits until they die. The longer the insured lives, the better the profits. The shorter the lifetime, the worse the profits. Those who die at a young age actually cause the insurance companies sizeable losses. What makes the system work is predictable mortality figures. AIDS and other high-risk diseases undermine this stability.

No one is suggesting that the insurance industry as a whole is insolvent. However, the next ten years are crucial as the big companies try to adjust to the declining real estate market and the impact that AIDS will have on our population. There will be many marginal insurance companies that will fail—leaving life, health, disability, and retirement annuities in default.

The Social Security side of retirement is detrimental to our economy.

Since many businesses' retirement accounts are actually underwritten by insurance company annuities, this potentially will leave millions of people totally dependent on Social Security alone. I believe that is a risky dependency.

TREMOR NUMBER 4: RETIREMENT ACCOUNTS

Our generation is emotionally dependent on retirement. We have come to expect retirement as an "entitlement," unlike any generation before us. To some extent retirement is beneficial, particularly at a time when most people live longer, because through retirement older workers cycle out of the economy and make way for younger ones.

But that small benefit is negated by the loss of millions of mature workers who, although they may not be able to work harder, certainly have learned to work smarter. However, this book is not on the advisability of retirement, so I will focus on the economic impact of retirement.

The truth is, large-scale retirement is extremely expensive and becomes impossible to fund on a current basis from Social Security taxes. A large reserve is needed from which retirement benefits can be drawn since there will not be sufficient current income to cover expenses in the next decade. The Social Security Trust Fund established to meet this need is a farce; there is no money in the fund—only government IOUs.

The more logical element in Congress has long realized that Americans had better put something aside for their latter years. The private retirement accounts were designed to do just that.

The funds being put into *private* retirement accounts are beneficial from two aspects. They are a form of voluntary savings, and the majority of these funds are reinvested into the economy. It is the very success of private retirement plans that may be their downfall.

The Social Security side of retirement is detrimental to our economy—both short term and long term. As of 1991, the Social Security "contributions" nearly equal the total personal income taxes paid by all American workers. The impact of this on the economy is staggering, especially when you consider that the annual Social Security surpluses, now averaging some $30 billion a year, are going to feed the annual budget deficits. This strips the economy of badly needed resources. The long-term impact may be even more devastating because millions of Americans are totally dependent on Social Security to meet their retirement goals. This it cannot do simply because the tax base is declining in proportion to the retirement base. Simply put, there will be too many retirees for the workers to support.

With some minor changes to the system, such as making Social Security an annuity-type plan, we could free as much as $200 billion a year to expand our economy, create more jobs, and develop a reliable retirement system.

An annuity-type system is very simple: Each participant is required to purchase an annuity for future benefits. Therefore, no one could draw out more than he had paid in. The system would be fair and totally funded—in advance. A thirty-year contributor would draw more than *twice* the present retirement benefit "promised" by Social Security, with no restrictions on other earned income. But I suppose the obvious is too simple.

Two significant problems loom large in the Social Security system: the increasing age of the American workers, and the increasing cost of providing health care for retirees.

Out of the $402 billion paid into Social Security in 1991 by active workers, $269 billion went to retirement benefits, $104.5 billion went to Medicare, and $28.5 billion was spent in the general revenue fund to pay the government's bills.

According to the Grace Commission's report, the Social Security system will need approximately $1.8 trillion a year to fund retirement and Medicare by the year 2000. Assuming a "normal" inflation rate of approximately 6 percent, the shortfall will be about $400 billion annually—in just nine years! Even if the government was saving the surpluses now, which it is not, the annual deficits would still run in excess of $300 billion. That does not take into account the escalating costs of health care that we have seen during the last five years.

WHERE WILL THE MONEY COME FROM?

The answer to this question should concern any thinking American. There are actually two potential sources of new entitlement funds (other than printing the money): increased taxes and private retirement accounts.

We will see Social Security taxes raised to 25 percent of gross wages, with no income cap.

Before discussing the source of new revenue for Social Security, let me describe some of the problems with our system.

There are millions of retired ex-federal employees drawing not only their federal retirement income but also Social Security benefits. The system is designed so that a retired worker from a career field not covered under the Social Security system can work for an additional ten years in a career that is covered, pay into Social Security the minimum contribution required, and draw benefits for a lifetime. With a contribution of no more than $7,000, a retired government employee can draw as much as $120,000 from the system, not including Medicare benefits.

Those who can qualify include members of the Congress (whose federal wages were exempt from Social Security), retired military personnel, federal government retirees, state government retirees, and exempt nonprofit organization employees (hospitals, churches, and the like). Many of these groups were brought under the Social Security system in the 1986 tax changes, but millions of previously exempt workers are now approaching retirement. By the time the workers who have paid into the system all their lives retire (from the year 2000 on) the system will be broke—twice over.

I said there were two methods to raise the needed funds to maintain the system through the end of this decade. Actually there is a third that the government has already opted to use once. It is the process of changing the rules, otherwise known as "pull the ladder up after you reach the top."

"But they can't do that," you say. "We have a contract with the government that says we can retire at age sixty-two or sixty-five, as we elect."

Well, your contract was just renegotiated, without you being a part of the "negotiation." As of 1986, workers born after 1938 had the retirement age raised by two years. However, as you might expect, the federal retirement program was not changed. Basically our politicians voted the change only for their constituents. I personally don't really mind. In the first place, I don't plan to retire until I am unable to get out of bed; and second, I would vote for the immediate retirement of all politicians if I could. It would be a lot cheaper in the long run.

Based on the need to further modify Social Security retirement, I believe it is quite possible that we will see the minimum retirement age raised to seventy before the end of this decade.

I also believe we will see Social Security taxes raised to 25 percent of gross wages, with no income cap. Basically, employers and employees will "voluntarily" contribute 25 percent of all earned income to the system. This will raise another $600 billion a year to feed both Social Security and the growing deficit. If the trust funds were intact, it is quite possible that the system would support the retirees who were born before 1938. By 2000 they will be sixty-two or older. For the rest of us, we will continue to work to provide the system with the money it will consume annually. By the year 2000 there will be only 3.2 workers for every retiree. In 1960 there were 14 workers for every retiree.

The last alternative is one I believe will be necessary to continue the system. Bear in mind that all of these suppositions assume a growing, viable economy. At present all the facts point to anything but that. If millions of workers are unemployed, the shortfalls in every category will become much larger.

---

*It is very likely that private
retirement accounts will
ultimately be absorbed into
the Social Security system.*

Although the federal government has not seen fit to store the surplus funds paid into the Social Security system, there is a large larder of funds available. It's called private retirement accounts.

There is approximately $600 billion stored in private IRAs. When the 401Ks, HR-10s, annuities, and the like are added to this, it is quite possible the total may reach $1.5 trillion. That great hoard of money will simply be too tempting for the politicians to pass up (in my opinion). It is very likely that private retirement accounts will ultimately be absorbed into the Social Security system and their owners given "equivalent" benefits.

Obviously this would be illegal and contrary to all contract law. But precedent indicates that the law is ignored when it is economically expedient to do so. Our look at recent actions verifies this fact. The rules were changed when necessity dictated it. You can be assured that this vast store of money in the hands of the "wealthy" has not been overlooked in the strategy of our policy makers.

Perhaps I am wrong. I sincerely hope so. But I personally would not do my planning based on either Social Security or tax-deductible retirement accounts.

It is also possible that before the need for retirement funds gets acute, the need for more spending in the economy will get larger. If so, the laws governing the use of retirement funds for education, buying homes, or even automobiles will be changed. If they are, I would suggest using those retirement account funds in place of current income to buy a home or educate your children. Then take your current income, pay the taxes, and store it for retirement. We are a long way from the confiscation of personal assets, but remember that tax-deferred funds are not yours: they are a gift from the government (at least in their thinking). The more indigestible (unable to absorb) you make your retirement funds, the safer they will be. Basically the Social Security system can't use your house, your cars, or your kids.

THE HEALTH CARE DEFICITS

The last area I want to discuss, in terms of deficits, is the huge black hole called "health care." At present the federal government is involved in health care only to the extent of military retirees' health care and Medicare benefits associated with Social Security. The Medicaid program is supported primarily by the states at this time, with some shared funds from the federal government.

Both federal and state health care costs are escalating out of control. Medicare now costs over $104 billion a year; up from $39 billion a decade ago. It is estimated (without the impact of AIDS) that federally supported health care costs will be more than $1.3 trillion by the year 2000.

When the costs of Medicaid (health services for the low-income families) are included, the total cost of government-provided health care represents nearly 30 percent of all taxes paid. Because of this and the escalating costs of private insurance, it seems certain that we will adopt some form of government-sponsored health insurance over the next few years. The 34 million Americans not covered by any kind of health insurance have virtually nowhere else to turn.

Having counseled many people in this situation, I can testify to the trauma that the lack of any health care insurance causes. If the church would wake up to its God-given mandate to care for the truly *needy*, we could provide adequate health care at a fraction of what a government program will eventually cost. Unfortunately, Christianity is not very well organized when it comes to cooperative efforts. The denominational and ideological barriers we erect keep us divided and our resources scattered. Consequently the government steps in to provide what is missing. With only twelve cents of every government dollar allocated to meet needs actually reaching the recipient, it is a grossly inefficient system.

There are two old sayings in Washington that describe what will happen to health care as soon as the political system gains control of that area too: "A camel is a horse designed by a government committee," and "An elephant is a mouse designed to government specifications." Unfortunately, these humorous quips have an uneasy ring of truth about them.

> *What our government does not seem to grasp is that businesses don't pay taxes. They simply pass along the added costs to consumers.*

As I noted earlier, when the Great Society under President Lyndon Johnson initiated the welfare system in 1964, it was supposed to eliminate poverty in twenty years and cost no more than $60 billion a year—at the very most. Here we are three decades later, and poverty is more widespread than ever, and the welfare program costs more than *$300 billion* a year! Of that, approximately one-third goes to health-related costs.

The only reasonable estimates I have been able to find on the potential costs of a government health insurance program that would cover all eligible Americans is approximately $180 billion a year (initially).

This represents additional spending above Medicare and Medicaid. Some cost reductions would be realized by the present system, so costs might drop by as much as $25 to $30 billion a year. What is the probable source of funding? Business taxes.

Unfortunately, what our government does not seem to grasp is that *businesses don't pay taxes.* They simply pass along the added costs to consumers. If the laws change to prohibit passing these costs along (as some politicians suggest), then the businesses will simply pack up and move to more amenable countries to make their products. Small businesses that cannot do this will end up in bankruptcy. Then we will lose the tax revenues they generate and add more people to the entitlements system.

AIDS

The cost of lifetime care for a symptomatic AIDS patient is approximately $175,000 at the present time. Thus the care of ten AIDS patients represents a cost of $1.75 million; 100 patients represent a cost of $17,500,000; 1,000 patients represent a cost of $175,000,000. It is estimated that there will be at least 4 million symptomatic patients in the United States in this decade. Factor that cost into the national health care system, and the economic effects are catastrophic.

Let's assume the estimates are off by 300 percent and only one million Americans develop symptomatic AIDS (exclusive of those with AIDS now immigrating to the U.S.). The total cost by the year 2000 will be at least $175 billion. Since most of the costs fall toward the end of this decade, we can expect some *$200* to *300 billion* a year to be spent caring for AIDS patients— just when our economy can least afford it.

Anyone who thinks these figures are exaggerated should talk with an administrator of a hospital that is treating AIDS patients. Perhaps a vaccine will be discovered that can stop the disease's progression. The taxpayers will bear that cost before this decade is out.

I am not trying to alarm anyone unnecessarily. I have simply presented the facts as we know them today. It is clear that we are having some severe economic tremors. These are merely the forewarning of some violent tremors to come before the "big quake" strikes. If my analysis is correct, we all need to make some radical adjustments—personally and "governmentally."

I know some will say this is an overreaction. I sincerely pray that it is, because my family and I have to live in this economy we have created. Along with all other Americans, I love this country and cherish the freedoms that we enjoy. History warns us that freedoms are often forfeited in bad economic times. We can't wait to see if the future will be a repeat of the past. Then it will be too late.

If my analysis (and that of many others) is correct, you and I had better be doing something in preparation right now—something pretty radical.

In the next chapter I would like to present the most likely scenarios of what our economy will look like through the end of this decade.

I am hesitant to do this because I realize how much of it is supposition. In a practical sense it is very difficult to determine what may or may not happen in a manipulated economy such as ours. I readily admit that I don't know exactly what will happen. All I can do is share what seems most logical in the midst of a totally illogical system. Please understand that events in our economy don't "just happen." There are some very intelligent men and women, employed full time by our government, who are trying to keep things going. Their decisions greatly affect the way our economy reacts to any crisis. What disturbs me the most is the apparent complacency about the ever-growing debt by politicians and public alike. This problem is so serious you would think there would be a bipartisan committee made up of Democrats and Republicans, senators and congressmen, liberals and conservatives, working night and day to balance the budget and reduce the debt. Instead, special interest groups keep vying for more handouts, and government economists testify that the debt is under control; control of what, I wonder?

It is true that with Americans hooked on the use of credit to buy virtually everything, an increase or decrease of two percentage points in interest rates can greatly affect buying habits, and even attitudes. Unfortunately attitude only goes so far. When families cannot pay their bills, no amount of cheap loans can resolve that problem. Americans may think economic controls will solve every problem; they won't. The controls we now have in place are like the rudder on that boat headed down the Niagara River. If the boat doesn't have the power to reverse course and avoid the falls, all the rudder operator can do is alter the path from side to side. Once the people in the boat hear the roar of the falls, the only choice left is which side of the falls to go over.

It is quite possible we will see a deflationary cycle in America as the consumer credit binge reaches its limits. If allowed to run its course, this deflation could help to restabilize our economy. But in the face of ever-increasing federal deficits and falling revenues, it is more likely that the government will resort to even more credit, creating a massive inflationary spiral.

The worst of all economic situations occurs when production falls while prices soar. This cycle, known as an inflationary-recession can rapidly deteriorate into a inflationary-depression in the hands of inept politicians.

11
Deflation or Inflation?

There is a strong argument in economic circles that the U.S. economy will enter a deflationary phase during which prices will actually fall and the economy will slow significantly. The winners in such an economy are those with cash and those who are debt free. In contrast, an inflationary economy benefits the borrowers and promotes greater indebtedness.

But why would anyone believe our bloated economy is going to deflate when there has been so much debt-funded expansion during the past two decades?

That is exactly why a period of deflation is anticipated. By and large, Americans are knowledgeable, independent-minded people. When they have exceeded their borrowing limits and sense a slowdown in the economy, they traditionally cut back on borrowing, concentrate on repaying some of what they owe, and generally get more conservative financially.

This trend has changed somewhat because a whole generation has been born into prosperity (and indebtedness), and unfortunately a whole generation has been raised to expect government handouts. But for the most part, many traditional values still exist within the younger generation too.

In spite of the alarming statistics on personal bankruptcies, most Americans will sacrifice to repay their debts, including selling unnecessary assets in bad times if required.

You don't have to look much farther than Texas to see what can happen to home prices during a severe economic slowdown.

Several factors point toward a period of deflation in our economy.

First, we have just about pushed the limit on debt-funded housing. Over the past two decades home prices have escalated to the point that the average home buyer cannot afford to buy the average home. To provide the extra income needed to qualify for the more costly homes, many women made a mass exodus from their homes to the work place during the seventies and eighties. But this has leveled off now, and a lot of women are opting to settle for less expensive houses so they can stay home with their children.

If this trend continues as expected, home prices should drop over the next few years or at least level out to some degree. This should result in a deflationary period for the second largest industry in our country. It will be good news for new buyers, but bad news for those using their homes as revolving lines of credit.

You don't have to look much farther than Texas to see what can happen to home prices during a severe economic slowdown. I know a couple who exemplify what can happen to anyone.

Cal and Andrea lived in Houston, Texas, where Cal managed a retail department store. Andrea worked for an attorney specializing in legal work for the oil industry.

Prior to the Arab oil embargo in the early seventies, Cal and Andrea had lived in Oklahoma, where Cal managed a similar but smaller store. When oil prices shot up and the Texas economy expanded rapidly, Cal's company asked him to relocate to Houston to manage a new store. He accepted the offer, and since the new position involved a bigger store and a higher salary he and Andrea felt they could afford a better home.

They moved to Houston in 1974 and purchased a four-bedroom, three-bath home in a nice neighborhood for $157,000. By 1975 the booming economy in Houston had driven the price of similar homes in their area up to nearly $250,000. Virtually every home was sold before construction was finished.

They borrowed against the equity in their home to install a swimming pool and landscape the property. Even so, the combined mortgages were only $190,000, and the payments were well within their combined incomes.

Then in 1980 disaster struck the oil industry as prices fell to pre-embargo levels. Cal noticed a significant drop in the volume of his store, even though it was a well-established discount store. The parent company was also shocked by the drop in sales, so prices were slashed to near break-even levels in an attempt to ride out what everyone believed was a temporary situation.

Deflation can be a great asset for those with cash to invest.

By 1982 it was apparent that the oil business in general was in trouble and the decline would not be as temporary as everyone had thought. Cal was fortunate because the parent company he worked for had the resources to ride out the downturn and was willing to do so, so he kept his job. But Andrea was not as fortunate; her employer was directly tied to the oil business, and in early 1983 she lost her job.

With the drop in income and few comparable positions available, they decided they had to sell their home. They both knew the Houston real estate market was down, but neither had any idea just how bad it was. They put their home on the market for $240,000 and had absolutely no offers. In fact, they had no lookers.

Over the next year they reduced the price several times, until they reached their break-even point on the outstanding loans: $190,000. Still they had no offers and very few lookers.

Andrea decided to do some checking on her own, so she began to call about some of the homes for sale in their community. What she discovered shocked her. The average price of a comparable home being offered (by the owner) was $140,000. But similar homes being offered by those who had already moved out of the state to find work averaged about $110,000.

Although bargains, these were not the lowest priced homes being offered. Foreclosed homes similar to theirs were being offered by the mortgage companies for as little as $80,000! In addition, the lenders were offering discounted interest rates, additional home equity loans—even trips to the Bahamas to qualified buyers.

By the end of 1983, long before the economy of Texas began a gradual turnaround, average home prices in their community dropped to as low as $100,000. But by 1985, if Cal and Andrea had been able to return their home to the mortgage company, they could have bought a similar home for $40,000 with a fifteen-year, 8 percent mortgage and only 10 percent down . . . and it had a larger pool.

Deflation can be a great asset for those with cash to invest. I know of an investor who bought dozens of homes in the Texas and Oklahoma area during this period. The homes he paid $40,000 or less for are now selling for $100,000 or more. Prices still have not returned to the pre-crash level and probably will not for several years, but the economy has returned to some semblance of normalcy.

THE MECHANICS OF DEFLATION

The second deflationary factor occurs when prices exceed the ability of the average consumer to buy what is offered. Demand can be artificially stimulated by lowering interest rates until consumers are enticed to buy again, in which case they are buying based on the perceived value of the loan, *not* necessarily the product. The "no interest" car loans of the late eighties are a good example of this. Many people bought cars they couldn't afford, simply because the loan was perceived as too good to pass up.

If allowed to run its full course, a deflationary spiral in the U.S. would wipe out millions of jobs. In the case of the deflation in Texas, there were jobs elsewhere for many of the displaced workers since the overall U.S. economy was doing well. But in a nationwide deflation, there would be widespread unemployment. Often the jobs that are available during a deflationary period are lower-paying, public service jobs. These types of jobs help to keep food on the table, but they won't pay the mortgage payments for most families.

A look at the most recent deflationary cycle will help give a better perspective of what happens when the downturn is broader and more pronounced.

As noted earlier, the 1980s saw the greatest credit-generated boom in American history. Businesses borrowed to expand; the government borrowed to expand; and consumers borrowed to expand. The automobile industry is a classic example of what can be called "smoke and mirrors" economics.

By the mid-eighties automobile prices had escalated to the point that most average buyers could not afford a new car. To overcome consumers' reluctance to spend more than they could afford, the automobile industry introduced "no interest loans." Anyone with common sense knows that you don't get something for nothing, so the industry had to build enough profit into the car prices to cover the loss of interest. But buyers did respond, and car sales soared. When Ronald Reagan left office, the great debt binge of the eighties slowed greatly. Buyers woke up to the fact that they had to pay their "no interest" car loans back. Consequently car sales plummeted, adding to the recession of 1990.

Assuming that the consumer debt-expansion cycle is slowing down, if not ending, then it is possible the economy will experience a period of deflation. However, because of the American consumer's addiction to credit, it is also quite possible that they will respond to yet another cycle of low interest rate stimuli by the government. If the Fed were to allow interest rates to drop to 6 percent or less, most Americans would respond by buying new cars, homes, boats, motorhomes, second homes, and other luxuries.

The unknown quantity in any situation is public attitude. During President Reagan's administration, Americans felt confident that the country had strong leadership, so they relaxed and spent money. That confidence may or may not hold firm in the future. One certainty is that most Americans have little confidence in the leadership of Congress. It is a peculiar relationship that keeps Americans voting for the very politicians they rate lowest on the respectability scale, and then voting in an opposition president to keep them in check.

BOTTOMING OUT

At the time of this writing it appears the 1990 recession is coming to an end. It is possible that we will have a "twin-dip" recession, meaning that the economy may improve and then dip again. This also is not some mystical economic phenomenon. It is the public's reaction to the "confidence" factor.

---

*The recession of 1990-1991
is not the signal of a
major economic depression.*

When the economy improves and Americans think there is reason to believe the government is making positive strides to resolve some of its problems, they start buying durable goods (houses, cars, refrigerators, and other items). If they have no confidence in the direction taken, they simply return to the previous conservatism and the economy dips again.

To counter this, the government can use the Federal Reserve system to force interest rates down. Whether or not this tactic works truly does depend on public confidence. Public confidence is that indefinable element that simply means, do we "think" things are getting better?

Since politics is so intertwined with our economy, the public often lays the blame (or applause) for economic performance at the feet of the president. Just as the manager of a team is rewarded for (or replaced because of) the record of his team, so are presidents. This provides a strong incentive for the incumbent to "stimulate" the economy. It is this scenario that tempts the administration to force interest rates below what may be prudent and stimulate the economy too quickly. Too much stimulation can result in higher inflation.

In my opinion, the recession of 1990-1991 is not the signal of a major economic depression. I believe we have at least one more cycle left in our economy (possibly two) before we face the real test.

The mid-1990s may well yield a growth spurt during which an attempt will be made to outrun inflation. Such an action could easily spark hyperinflation. This philosophy would conform nicely with the previous patterns leading up to a major depression.

Assuming a three- or four-year period of stimulation (debt expansion) the stage would be set for another recession in the latter half of this decade. Depending on whether or not this downturn comes before or after an election year will greatly determine the response by the incumbent administration.

Project yourself into the future a little and try to visualize what the economy might be like through the remainder of the nineties (assuming no major wars, oil embargoes, or other unforeseen calamities occur).

I am going to make some "assumptions" at this point, because accurate forecasting is not possible so far in advance.

1993-1995 will probably be the era of massive new social programs.

I will assume that the recession of 1990 "officially" ends by the first quarter of 1992—just in time for the presidential election. Bear in mind that even after a recession "officially" ends, the economy doesn't resume its former course as if nothing had ever happened. Many companies plan their work force at least a year in advance, so reductions in personnel may continue even after the economy recovers some steam. Also, retailers usually sell 20 percent or more of their yearly volume in December, so if they miss the Christmas season they will not expand again until the next season. Depending on the timing of a recovery, the statistical indicators may say a recession is over, but the average unemployed workers may not be able to tell the difference.

If my assumptions are accurate, by late 1992 or early 1993 the economy should be "perking" again, and since many of the previous three-year car notes will have been paid off (or the cars repossessed), the automobile companies should be looking at an improving economic situation.

Even with a reluctant president, 1993-1995 will probably be the era of massive new social programs, including (but not limited to) some form of national health care, low-income tax credits, subsidized day care, and whatever else the Congress can get past the president. I also assume the Democrats will concede the presidency for four more years, but will concentrate on acquiring the votes to override the vetoes to their social programs. It is entirely possible we will see annual budget deficits in the *trillion* dollar range before this decade ends.

Once the economy has fully recovered from the recession, I rather suspect that our less-than-conservative politicians will sell the public on more debt to fund their social programs. I can already hear the politicians' appeals on the evening news: "It's clear that the alarmists were wrong about the debt. The economy has recovered, and now we need to get on with the business of government: meeting needs. I recommend that we raise the allowable budget deficit to $6 quadrillion. . . ." This should carry us well into the late mid-nineties, with inflation becoming an increasingly nagging problem. I believe the price declines of the previous three or four years will be forgotten as inflation sparks again.

The single effective control for inflation is recession and, as I said before, in a debt-run economy like ours the primary retardant is higher interest rates. Almost certainly, higher interest rates will be employed in an attempt to control inflation.

It is my assumption that some event will initiate a massive spending cutback on the part of consumers. This could be a stock market crisis or an oil embargo, but more likely it will be the collapse of several "mega-banks," insurance companies, or large corporations.

Remember what was mentioned earlier: There is no way to determine timing so far in advance. These events could occur in the mid-nineties or the latter part of this decade. It is always possible that some calamity could spark a panic at any time. The important thing to remember is that no economy can sustain the debt-growth cycle indefinitely.

One day the nation will experience the ravages of hyperinflation.

It is hard to imagine at this time that our politicians might actually decide to stop their mad spending and balance the nation's budget. This would surely result in a prolonged period of economic stagnation that would be politically unpopular. Therefore, I have discounted such a ridiculous notion.

At some point the economy must come a full circle: recession to inflation to recession. Then an administration that has pledged itself to no recessions will be facing a possible depression. When that happens I assume all the stops will be pulled and whatever is necessary will be done, including "monetizing" the debt (printing new money).

At first the amount of fiat money issued probably will be just enough to cover the deficits that cannot be funded through increased taxes and new loans. But as the need grows, so will the printing of money. One day the nation will experience the ravages of hyperinflation, and the attention of the media will shift from stimulating the economy to slowing the price spiral. Americans will face the most difficult of conditions with a depressed economy and soaring prices.

Once the international business community loses confidence in the dollar, the European Community may well step in with the Eurodollar to stabilize the world's exchange system. Simply put, the dollar will no longer be the world's trading currency; the Eurodollar will be.

Once the economy begins the "stagflation" spiral, which punishes both creditors and debtors, angry voters will demand action from the government. It has often been suggested that major riots could erupt as frustrated unemployed workers vent their anger on their own cities.

Very possibly the business community will demand and receive import restrictions on foreign goods in an attempt to secure their home market. This same mentality surfaced in 1930 as American manufacturers saw all foreign importers as unwelcome competitors. Unfortunately this sparked an international trade war that plunged the whole world into depression. With Americans totally dependent on many foreign products, trade restrictions would greatly inflate prices because of the import tariffs. In the long run everybody loses, as when artificial trade barriers are raised, but to placate those facing the loss of their jobs the politicians need a scapegoat; foreign competitors become appealing targets. In reality American businesses have the most to lose because the Japanese have moved much of their production to the U.S. and other countries benefiting from our "most favored nation" policy. While they will have access to our markets, we will lose any access to theirs.

Those living in earthquake regions would do well to pay attention to the early indicators of a major earthquake. Those living on the edge of an economic earthquake should heed the warnings of that calamity as well.

Our political leaders are digging an ever-widening financial pit that may one day swallow them and us.

12
Early Indicators

I need to emphasize once again that there are no "absolutes" when it comes to economic forecasting. We live in a society where few people want to live by absolutes themselves but they want others to provide them with absolute answers. If that's what you expected when you picked up this book, I'm sorry, but you're going to be disappointed. I think I can offer some guidelines or indicators of what to look for in our economy, but absolutes are the sole realm of God.

POSITIVE INDICATORS

It is a possibility, however remote, that our government leaders will recognize the dangerous path they are on and decide to get fiscally responsible.

I don't mean to imply that no one in Washington understands the crisis we face or wants to do anything about it. There are many financially conservative politicians who also believe the government is on a collision course with disaster and needs to change immediately. Unfortunately they are a minority and are often characterized by the more fiscally liberal politicians as uncaring right-wingers, which in itself is ridiculous because many of these people are among those labeled as socially liberal themselves by most political conservatives.

Representative among this group are two recently retired politicians: Congresswoman Millicent Fenwick and Senator William Proxmire. No one has ever accused either of them of being "conservatives," but both spoke out strongly against waste and debt during their tenure in Washington.

POSITIVE INDICATOR 1: INITIATE SPENDING CUTS

If the Congress decides to follow the law as set down by the Gramm-Rudman Act and bring the federal budget into balance, you will know that the economy is headed down the path to recovery. Because of the enormity of the deficits, this will require across-the-board cuts in *every* budget area, including "entitlements." There is simply no way to bring the budget into balance and exclude 70 percent of current spending. This action would bring those in Congress who are dedicated to the redistribution of wealth screaming to the media. In my opinion, the political nature of this issue makes implementation almost impossible.

POSITIVE INDICATOR 2: STOP THE "PORK BARREL" POLITICS

If the Congress allows the president a line-item veto so that he can reject specific areas of overspending without rejecting the entire budget, you will know they're serious about solving the problems.

It is often too easy to blame the Congress for everything because they are the "big" spenders.

As it is now, the Congress attaches hundreds of special-interest appropriation bills to the budget. The budget is usually associated with a politically sensitive issue, such as civil rights or aid for dependent children. Then the politicians sit on the appropriations bill until midnight before the federal government's funds run out, sending it to the White House at the "twelfth" hour. The president is then confronted with either signing a budget that he doesn't agree with or shutting down the government and facing the wrath of angry citizens. If the politicians decide to stop this "pork barrel" method of funding their special projects, you'll know they are serious.

POSITIVE INDICATOR 3: STOP
THE DIVERSION OF NON-BUDGET FUNDS

If the president decides to stop robbing funds from Social Security and allow the budget to reflect the true deficits, including the off-budget entitlement programs, you will know the executive branch is also serious about solving the country's economic problem.

> *We have a system that bogs down
> under stress and leaders who are
> more concerned with avoiding the
> blame than solving the problems.*

It is often too easy to blame the Congress for everything because they are the "big" spenders. But the executive branch of our political system has pushed its pet projects too, including billion dollar airplanes with dubious performance and $500 hammers. When you see members of the White House staff driving their own cars to work and flying the commercial airlines like the rest of us, then you'll know the executive branch is serious too.

POSITIVE INDICATOR 4: FORM A
GOVERNMENT/BUSINESS PARTNERSHIP TO EXPAND EXPORTS

One economic factor that could signal an improving market for American goods is the expansion into eastern Europe by American businesses. This vast untapped market lacks the capital to buy many Western goods presently. But they will certainly emerge as a viable economic force before the end of this century, bringing 100 million new and willing consumers on line.

This market base could enhance the U.S. economy to the point where we could absorb the present debt (assuming the politicians stop future waste). If the U.S. waits, we will find ourselves trying to catch up with the Asians in Europe, as we have in our own country. By the end of the century the Russians should have recovered sufficiently to be formidable competitors also.

At present I see no concerted effort by the Congress or the president to provide incentives for American businesses to expand into this marketplace. If the government merely allowed tax-free earnings for investments in businesses that market to eastern Europe, we would lose nothing and possibly gain the edge needed to outflank the Japanese. Unfortunately, in political language this means helping the "rich" again because they would directly benefit from the tax incentives. Apparently the Japanese have no such misgivings, so they provide incentives for the rich to invest in export industries. If you don't think it has helped the average Japanese workers also, just look at who makes your television set, VCR, video camera, and half of your neighbors' cars.

NEGATIVE INDICATORS

While I sincerely pray that our leaders will show enough statesmanship and courage to make these changes and more, I seriously doubt that our political system will support such an effort.

No long-range changes are possible unless some short-range sacrifices are made by the American people. I question that our generation has the will and determination (or foresight) to back those who would do what is best in the long run.

Perhaps I am wrong. I sincerely pray that I am because I live in this country too. However, to date I have not seen many leaders with the integrity of a Grover Cleveland or an Abraham Lincoln, who will do what is best for the country regardless of the political consequences.

The decisions that must be made, once the cracks in the economy begin to widen, require swift and positive leadership. In my opinion, we have a system that bogs down under stress and leaders who are more concerned with avoiding the blame than solving the problems. As a result, when the real economic tremors begin, it will be too late to do much about it. The mentality of my fellow Americans truly astounds me sometimes. Even with the massive debt already accumulated and annual deficits now doubling every five years, there is no real clamor for change. Apparently the average American has either bought the nonsense that the debt doesn't matter, or they simply don't care.

I trust that some do, and that you are one of them. The collapse of this economy truly will come like "a thief in the night." Trying to bolt the doors after the thief is inside is a rather fruitless effort.

CRACK NUMBER 1: THE DEFICIT CANNOT
BE FUNDED BY ADDITIONAL BORROWING

Up to the time of this writing, our government has been able to avoid the consequences of hyperinflation because the annual deficits have been funded through loans.

---

*Once the limit to which
foreign investors will fund
the U.S. debt is reached,
a monetary crisis is not far off.*

Some inflation does occur even when the deficits are funded this way because the fractional banking system creates some new money, based on the multiplier effect previously discussed. However, the amount of fiat money this system can create is insignificant in comparison to the deficits of the federal government. The fractional banking system is limited to multiplying only the deposits on hand. As these dry up, the money supply shrinks proportionately. The net result is a nagging 4 or 6 percent inflation rate, which is bad but not when compared with that of the other countries we discussed who simply printed the money they needed.

Two points must be noted here. First, the countries where hyperinflation ignited so quickly lacked the established credit rating of the United States. Hence, they simply had to start printing money to cover their deficits much sooner.

The second point is that *any* debt-funded economy will eventually exhaust its available credit. If allowed to grow unchecked, the annual deficits will exceed the total funds available from all sources.

The beginning of the real economic crisis in our country will come when the deficits reach the point where the funds cannot be raised through loans. It is important to understand that there is a finite amount of money to be loaned from all sources. In the early eighties the U.S. government exceeded the amount that could be raised from its citizens alone and became dependent on foreign sources of credit. Now nearly 20 percent of the annual deficit is funded by foreign investors, and almost $300 billion of the total national debt is owned directly by foreign investors. Perhaps as much as $600 billion is controlled through foreign-owned financial entities (banks, businesses, and the like).

Once the limit to which foreign investors will fund the U.S. debt is reached, a monetary crisis is not far off. Two factors can create this crisis. First, the foreign investors may see the U.S. government as a bad risk. This does not necessarily mean they believe the government is going under; it may just be that the value of the dollar is falling faster than the return on their investment.

For instance, let's assume a Japanese investor places $100,000 in U.S. T-bills at 10 percent per year for three years. Then during that period the dollar is devalued 10 percent annually, compared to the Japanese yen. The net effect for our Japanese investor is zero return on his investment. If the dollar falls more than 10 percent per year against the yen, he actually loses money. Benevolence only goes so far in international finances, and this investor will cease to lend more under these circumstances.

One solution to this crisis is to pay a higher rate of return for T-bills held by foreign investors. In other words, index the rate of return to the devaluation of our dollar. Unfortunately this has the undesirable side effect of increasing the deficit even more and accelerating the decline of the dollar. It is another of those Catch 22s.

Also if the government bankers offer too high a rate of return, they will drive up interest rates for everyone, including the businesses competing for some of the same dollars. This will force businesses to pay even higher rates of return, weakening their financial structure.

The competition between the government and businesses for available funds is a real concern to most economists who understand that the total funds available to both the public and private sector are limited. The more money the government pulls out of the system to feed its own spending, the less that is available for businesses. Since only the government can support the enormous deficits it has, businesses are in constant jeopardy of losing their source of capital.

The following graph depicts the needs of businesses and government for annual loans. As you can see, the more the government siphons off, the less that is available for all others. The law of supply and demand eventually comes into play, and the price of credit climbs beyond the reach of the productive side of our economy.

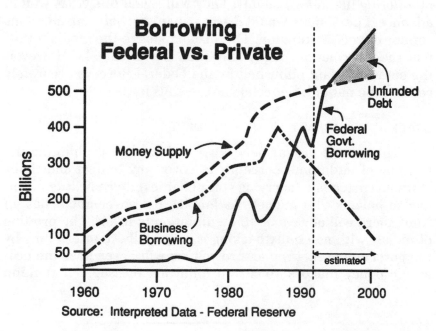

Borrowing - Federal vs. Private

Source: Interpreted Data - Federal Reserve

Based on the projected deficits, this point will be reached sometime in the latter part of this decade. Unless the government reduces its demand for capital, the business base of American industry will eventually be forced to sell out to foreign investors to acquire the needed funds.

This is one of the indicators I mentioned earlier. When the annual deficits (on budget and off) reach the level where the government can no longer fund them without taking critical operating funds away from industry, the economic blow-off is not far away.

The printing of money with no equity backing is essentially counterfeiting by the government.

How can you know when this is happening? Just read the financial section of *The Wall Street Journal* or *Investor's Daily*, or listen to the financial news on a non-network channel. I can assure you there are professional analysts who make their living monitoring the money supply. They will signal this crisis well in advance. I personally would disregard any verbal contradictions coming out of Washington. This also applies to the media if they feel the information might hurt their social agenda. However, the statistical data published by the Federal Reserve accurately reflects the nation's financial status—thus far.

CRACK NUMBER 2: MONETIZING THE DEBT

There is an urgent need for a federal law prohibiting the printing of additional currency to cover any budget shortfalls. Without such a law (carrying stiff penalties) there is little incentive to balance the budget. As long as the government has an "out" there will always be the temptation to use it. The printing of money with no equity backing is essentially counterfeiting by the government. Let me assure you we will never hear the economic policy makers voice the following message: "Attention

Americans. Today we will start monetizing the national debt. You can expect extremely high levels of inflation to follow."

Instead, an innocuous term such as "monetary equalization" will be used. This is what George Orwell described as "government speak" in his novel *1984.*

We are usually told by campaigning politicians that no new taxes will be allowed while they are in office. Then a few months later, when you receive your tax bill, it looks like you owe more taxes this year than you did the last, but your income remained the same. Why?

The political explanation: You didn't have a tax increase; you experienced a "revenue enhancement." A revenue enhancement often means that we taxpayers lost some of the deductions so generously granted to us in previous years. The net effect is the same: More of our incomes are transferred to the government. A little later we'll look at some of the more probable revenue enhancers.

The treasury notes now in circulation have no real collateral behind them other than the holder's confidence in our government.

When debt is "monetized" it simply means that a new form of currency has been issued as legal tender. This was done in the 1700s when the fledgling American government issued script to replace the British pound. Later the highly devalued script was exchanged for the continental dollar. A few years later the continental dollar was so worthless, due to indiscriminate printing, that it was exchanged for U.S. gold or silver certificates. As long as the dollar was backed by these metals, there was very little inflation.

The New Deal administration exchanged the gold certificates for federal reserve notes, allowing the dollar to rise and fall, depending on the state of the economy.

Then in the sixties President Nixon substituted the use of base metal coins for silver coins, effectively removing all fixed asset value from U.S. currency.

So the precedent is well established for the additional monetizing of our currency. Only this time it will be the printing of a currency already in circulation: the dollar. Simply put, we will eventually be forced to print what we can't borrow.

The treasury notes now in circulation have no real collateral behind them other than the holder's confidence in our government. Those who hold U.S. dollars throughout the world are reasonably sure that the government will not print additional bills without removing the equivalent number from circulation. If they thought otherwise they (including you and I) would dump or trade our currency as quickly as possible. Because each new bill printed and put into circulation would make those we are holding worth less than before.

Think of the dollars you hold like stock in a company. Suppose a company with a total worth of $100,000 is authorized to issue 100 shares of stock. So you buy one share with assurance that it is worth $1,000, based on the current value of the company. Later the company needs more capital so the directors issue 100 more shares and sell them to the public for $1,000 a share.

At first glance, you might think, *Well it doesn't hurt me. I still have my share worth $1,000.*

But is it really worth $1,000? If the company is still valued at $100,000 and there are 200 shares outstanding, your share is only worth $500. However, it is possible that no one else knows that another 100 shares have been issued. The "logical" thing to do in that case is to dump your shares before the others discover the company has diluted your stock by 50 percent.

In the case of a public company that did this, the directors would be subject to both civil lawsuits and criminal prosecution because they violated the securities law and the trust agreement with their original stockholders. It is unfortunate that the same rules do not apply to governments and their dollar holders.

The current method of funding the government's debt is that the Treasury issues loan agreements (T-bills, bonds, and the like), which are sold through the federal reserve banks strategically located throughout the country. Since each issue from the Treasury is a sale of securities, the laws applicable to public information require total disclosure.

In the event the Treasury decides to print fiat money to pay the government's bills, you can be sure the action will be cloaked in secrecy and disguised as something else, contrary to the securities' laws. But I have confidence that the American free enterprise system will not allow such activities to go unnoticed or unreported.

It should be noted here that the printing of money to pay the government's bills will be one of the last, and certainly the most desperate, measures because of the potential severity of the consequences.

Additional taxes take away the ability to save for future generations.

On the other hand, the money managers may counsel that it's okay to print a little money along the way to ease the demand on the money supply.

I am reminded that eighty years ago the money managers promised that the federal income tax would never exceed 2 percent of earned income. If printing a little extra money generates raising a little extra tax, this crack will widen quickly.

CRACK NUMBER 3: TAXES, TAXES, TAXES . . .

When the American standard of living is compared to that of most other countries of the world, it is evident that we can support a much higher tax base. Even supporting a federal income tax of 50 percent would not require a reduction in living standards as much as it would a change of lifestyles. It would necessitate a return to one car per family, multiple generations per home, less education, one suit in the closet, and so on.

If we don't wake up and demand some changes, this is exactly where we are headed again. Additional taxes take away the ability to save for future generations.

Those who support a higher tax rate point out that not too long ago the maximum tax rate in our country was 70 percent and people still lived okay. What they miss is that most taxpayers didn't fall into the highest bracket and, in fact, the tax rate was designed specifically to encourage high income individuals to invest in the economy through the use of tax shelters.

Most certainly, average-income wage earners would balk at a tax rate of 50 percent or more, so it would need to be disguised. Allow me to share some creative ways to do this.

Gasoline Tax. A proposal that is raised frequently in the Congress is assigning a "user fee" to gasoline. The general consensus is about ten cents per gallon. An alternate suggestion is 10 percent fee per gallon, which would provide an inflation hedge (for the government of course). As the cost of gasoline went up, the fee would follow. This method of tax increase is called *indexing.*

A federal gasoline tax would raise an additional $15 to $20 billion annually. Because of its impact on the lower income groups, a new tax on gasoline would probably provide some form of tax credit based on income.

Value-Added Tax. Those who have traveled through England and Europe are familiar with the value-added tax system. It is a national tax (with local government participation) that is added to each stage of material production and distribution.

In the United States, no sales taxes are added until a product is sold to the consumer. Not so in the value-added system. Each recipient of raw materials or materials pays a tax. The raw materials sent to a processor are taxed. Then the processed materials are taxed to the manufacturer. They are taxed again when sold to the retailer. Another percentage is added when the products are sold to the consumers.

The value-added tax (on most products) can be as high as 40 percent when the totals are accumulated. Since the tax is paid by all classes of taxpayers, the income to the government is significantly greater than a graduated income tax. In countries such as England, France, and Germany, the income taxes may also total 40 percent or more. In some of the more socialized economies, such as Norway and Sweden, income taxes can be as much as 70 percent. Based on a complicated formula, some income is taxed at more than 100 percent. It is designed to be the optimum "soak the rich" tax.

A value-added tax on all goods and services in America could potentially add an additional $300 billion annually to the government's coffers. But it's important to remember that you don't get something for nothing. The $300 billion must be removed from the private sector economy to be given to the public sector. Doing so reduces the consumer's buying power and thus ripples through the entire economy.

What is the national debt but the visible indicator of gross fiscal mismanagement on the part of our leaders?

Visualize the tax system like a home builder who wants to economize on his construction costs by removing the wall studs one at a time to see how many are really necessary to keep the walls standing. If he removes one too many, the whole structure collapses.

The government is playing the same game with our tax base. If it removes too much private capital, the whole structure can collapse. Unfortunately the mentality of too many Americans today is that it would *never* do that.

A National Lottery. It would seem entirely plausible that the federal government will turn to a lottery of some kind when the need for more money becomes acute. Based on what the states are able to generate through their lotteries, a national lottery would net the government about $20 to $25 billion annually. If the government gets really creative and makes the proceeds tax free, the net could be as high as $100 billion.

I hesitate to mention a national lottery lest someone in Washington who had not already thought about it pick up on the idea. But I read in a national magazine that two of our more liberal senators had already proposed the idea. Raising money through gambling represents just one more small crack in the ever-expanding financial chasm.

The "success" of state lotteries in reducing taxes should forewarn everyone that lotteries *do not* reduce taxes. The net effect is an increase in income, but at the cost of morality and more welfare to compensate for the money the poor spend on gambling.

It is important to remember that more taxes are not a problem. They are the symptom of a greater internal problem: indulgence. A politician would rather do anything other than raise taxes. The escalating growth of the national debt is evidence of this. After all, what is the national debt but the visible indicator of gross fiscal mismanagement on the part of our leaders? But rather than facing irate voters by raising the money they spend, our leaders borrow the money and put off the inevitable one more year—or day.

So when you see an increase in taxes (other than a "soak the rich" tax) you know the politicians are desperate. The more visible the tax, such as the value-added tax, the more desperate they are for money. When they dip down into the pockets of the low-income groups through taxes on food, gasoline, and medicines, the end is nearing.

Unlike an earthquake that will often erupt unexpectedly, the economy gives fair warnings of an impending disaster. Unfortunately, most people don't heed the warnings and usually get caught unaware. A proverb says, "A wise man looks ahead and sees a problem and avoids it. A fool proceeds without caution."

When the interest on the national debt exceeds the total income of our government, it would be prudent to assume the system is about to "roll over."

13
The Final Warnings

In one study I read describing earthquakes, a group of scientists presented some convincing evidence that animals can be used as early warning detectors.

For instance, ants seem to sense the faint rumblings of an earthquake even before the most sensitive seismology equipment can. Ant colonies begin migrating away from the areas of eruption long before there is even a hint of geological activity. Of course, since many ant colonies are in constant migration, it is easy to overlook the obvious sometimes. Only by studying stable colonies have scientists begun to accept this theory as a possible indicator.

The same can be said of the economic indicators. After all, taxes are always in a state of flux. And our currency has been changed at least twice in this century. So why worry about these indicators? It is both the intensity and the combination of many factors converging that represent the best early warning indicators.

If I lived in an earthquake area I wouldn't be particularly concerned about a migrating colony of ants. But if I woke up one morning and noticed the majority of ants packing up to move, it would get my attention. I think I would question whether they knew something I didn't. From that point on, I would be on the alert for other indicators.

The same group of scientists who noted the movement of ants prior to major eruptions also noted that many species of birds vacate the area just prior to the actual earthquake. The birds either don't have the early warning sensitivity of the ants, or they know they can escape faster. But once the time draws near, apparently they can feel the low frequency rumblings preceding the actual eruption.

The general rule in predicting earthquakes is, The earlier the better. But the absolute rule is, Any warning is better than none at all. Applying this logic to our coming economic earthquake, I believe the earlier we can spot it coming, the better it will be for all of us, especially those who will *do something* in advance. But even those who choose to ignore all the early warning indicators will be attentive when the loud rumblings start. I might not be concerned if a few ants left the area, but if I woke up to find all the animals gone, that would get my attention. There are some people, however, who would say, "Good! The noisy varmints are gone!" and then roll over and go back to sleep.

Our economy will suffer a shattering depression during which the government will attempt to stimulate the economy by inflating the currency.

Those charged with the management of our economy will likely say, "That's ridiculous. There are no real problems with our economy. Roll over and go back to sleep." If you do, I believe your sleep will be rudely interrupted. As with a geological earthquake, there is little you can do once the earth begins to move, except flee your house for an open field somewhere close by. But even standing in an open field during a major quake is better than staying inside. Perhaps all you can do once the economy begins to crumble is save what you can of your assets (house, car, or the like) by paying them off; at least you'll be doing something.

Based on the study of other economic collapses, I believe there will be a series of crises prior to either a depression or hyperinflation. It is also my firm conviction that our economy will suffer a shattering depression during which the government will attempt to stimulate the economy by inflating the currency. This will then initiate a period of hyperinflation.

In order to understand how and why this can happen, we must project ourselves into the future and decide what we would do under the conditions that will be facing the president and Congress at that time. Remember, these are not "Supermen." Nor are they clairvoyant. They are men and women who make decisions based on the facts at hand and the political climate at the time. What Americans in the thirties expected of their government was far less than what is expected today. Ten years of depression left a lot of people disillusioned in the thirties. Today it would leave burned-out hulks of cities throughout America.

As I commented before, we're whipping our horse (the economy) to avoid the Indians chasing us (the debt). We realize if we keep inflating the economy at this pace it will collapse. But we also know that if the economy stops for any period of time, the debt will overwhelm us. So what can we do? Keep whipping our horse and hoping for a miracle.

When you see cracks appearing in the earth in an earthquake zone, the actual eruption is near. When you see cracks in the economy, you'll know that financial eruption is near also.

CRACK NUMBER 1:
BANKING CRISIS

We have discussed in part the potential of a banking crisis, but one of the signs of an imminent collapse is massive bank failures. Just in case you may not be aware that there is a banking crisis looming, I need to point out some facts.

Prior to 1991, interstate national banks were prohibited by law—this meant that one corporation could not own banks across the country. The logic behind this limitation is obvious: If one corporation controls banks throughout the country, it could eventually develop a monopoly and choke off the competition. Also if a nationwide banking corporation developed financial

problems it could threaten the whole banking system. Therefore, previous laws limited banks to regional ownership.

Mergers and buy-outs work only if the surviving entity is
financially stronger than those absorbed. That was not true with
the S&Ls, and it may not be true with the banks.

Larger banks do have access to the funds to buy out weaker
institutions simply because of their size. But their debt-to-asset
ratios are actually worse than many of the smaller banks. Unless
there are some genuine efforts to bring the big banks under control, when the real economic crunch comes they will simply go
under with a bigger bang.

---

*We are witnessing the conversion
of the entire banking industry
into a new financial entity.*

The second change the banking committee made was to allow non-banking corporations to own banks. This has opened
the door for large retailers like Sears, J. C. Penney, Wal-Mart,
K-Mart, and others to buy banks. Additionally, it paved the way
for insurance companies and stock brokerage firms to get into
the banking business. This idea would have been soundly rejected only a few years earlier.

The advantage to the non-banking corporations is obvious.
It gives them access to depositors' funds at extremely low rates
and access to the lucrative credit card business. For the insurance companies and brokerage firms, it provides a nationwide
outlet for their products through neighborhood banks.

The negative side is that it breaks down the barriers between depositors and financial product marketers. It also opens
the door to abuses by these companies for loans in self-interest.
This in turn can make the banks more vulnerable to problems in
the parent companies' industry.

In short it does provide an instant "shot in the arm" for the
banking industry, but it can easily destabilize the economy in the
long run. The only thing that makes such a move possible is the
federal depositors insurance program. Otherwise, nervous de-

positors would pull out of troubled banks, especially those making loans to their parent companies.

We are witnessing the conversion of the entire banking industry into a new financial entity. If these mergers and acquisitions strengthen the banks, the economy will benefit. But if the big, shaky banks simply gobble up the smaller, more conservative banks to get at their asset base, it can be a critical blow to the economy.

The "merger mania" of the eighties left many businesses in shambles and helped to create the very crisis that now necessitates bank mergers. Watch very closely the ratings of these new "mega-banks."

Banks are private companies that make their money in the lending business. If the majority of their loans are participating (making their payments) then they are solvent. Once the number of bad loans exceeds the statistical number necessary to repay the depositors' interest, the bank will fail without government intervention.

In a bad economy with unemployment exceeding 10 percent or more, many of the normally sound loans will default. This crack in the economy will be highly publicized because it will swallow up hundreds of banks, large and small, and will require a *trillion dollars* or more in additional government subsidies.

Once again the same question surfaces: Where will the funds come from at a time when the economy is flagging and the government's income is declining? The same three options are available: new taxes, more loans, or printed money. Take your pick.

CRACK NUMBER 2: BUSINESS FAILURES AND DEPARTURES

When all is said and done, the business community in our country is the heart of our economy. The single bright spot that I can see on the horizon is the ability of American entrepreneurs to adapt to virtually any situation and still make a profit.

The biggest negative is the excessive burden placed on them by our political system. It is very popular these days to attack business people as greedy money grubbers who need to be watched carefully and regulated heavily. If this trend continues, we will lose the base from which all of our capital is generated. Allow me to cite an example.

Some time ago a businessman I know called to say that he was relocating his business outside the U.S. The reason: the constant pressure from our government bureaucracy.

He owned a company in the western United States and a sizeable portion of his business was providing parts for catalytic convertors on automobiles. A part of the manufacturing process involved the use of a potent acid catalyst, which was recaptured, cleaned, and reused again.

Three years earlier he was required by the Environmental Protection Agency (EPA) to install some very expensive equipment to monitor the plant's environment to ensure that no workers were exposed to the caustic fumes. He did this willingly, believing it was in the best interests of his employees.

> *The EPA [has] become a paramilitary enforcement group running amuck throughout the free enterprise system.*

Recently he received a bill from the EPA for his "share" of an environmental cleanup. It seems the company he bought the monitoring equipment from also used toxic chemicals in their testing facility. The facility failed to meet EPA standards and was required to decontaminate their entire complex, which meant chipping out several hundred yards of concrete and storing it in sealed containers for the next 150 years or so. Rather than absorb these costs, the company, a subsidiary of a foreign firm, declared bankruptcy and closed its doors.

The EPA then sent a portion of the cleanup estimate to all the companies that had ever done business with the firm, including this businessman. The thing about it that bothered him the most was the only slightly veiled threat he received. The attorneys for the EPA warned him that if he refused to pay his "share," amounting to tens of thousands of dollars, he could be held liable for the entire cleanup, amounting to several millions of dollars. The timing was significant since he had just returned from an industry meeting where other business owners shared horror stories of similar conflicts with various government agencies; many of them had had their assets attached when they refused to comply.

"Enough is enough," he told me. "Government officials from another country want me to relocate my business there, and they've offered me tax breaks, low-interest loans, and governmental guarantees of *no* interference. I can see the handwriting on the wall here. So I'm going!"

He offered his employees a chance to relocate also. As expected, no one took the offer, so 1300 employees were out of a job, and another industry left the U.S.

I'm sure some newspaper or television station in his area will eventually do a report on the callous businessman who dumped his employees for a few dollars. But that was not the case at all. He grieved over his decision, and then he provided liberal benefits to those who were dismissed.

"My great concern," he said, "is that one day the rules will get so oppressive that I won't be able to operate profitably and laws will be passed to keep me from relocating. So I'm getting out while I still can." He saw the EPA in the same role as the KGB in Russia. They have become a paramilitary enforcement group running amuck throughout the free enterprise system.

The environment has become the new buzzword in Washington, and there is little doubt that more of this kind of activity will take place. Our system of regulation seems to swing from one extreme to the other—never reaching the proper balance.

When the additional factors of mandatory health insurance, workman's compensation, liability insurance, property taxes, inventory taxes and, eventually, value-added taxes are dumped on small and medium-sized businesses, we will see some massive failures.

The interdependent relationships between banks and businesses tend to feed each other. If one goes, the other is sure to follow.

As banks fail, the primary source of operating capital dries up for the local businesses. Then, as businesses fail, other banks are jeopardized because they have loaned to businesses that are dependent on the failed enterprises.

This may sound depressing, but perhaps making more people aware of the impending crisis will help to deal with the problems before the whole structure unravels.

CRACK NUMBER 3:
THE DENIAL SYNDROME

The one thing you can be certain of is that no one in the power structure of Washington will admit to any problems until the evidence is so overwhelming that it is obvious to all. It's like we're headed down the Niagara River in a powerless boat, and yet they still insist, "There is no problem. The sound you hear in the distance is not a waterfall. We promise!"

I heard Lee Iacocca say during an interview in the midst of the 1990 recession, "I know the politicians tell us that we're not in a recession and we're not going to be, but, from where I stand, it sure does look like a recession."

I agree with Mr. Iacocca. If it is in the best interests of the political system to deny a problem, they will do so in spite of overwhelming evidence to the contrary. The more vehement the denials, the bigger the potential crisis.

Even if the evidence indicates bank failures, business failures, and desperate efforts on the part of federal and state governments to raise funds, you can be sure the information coming out of Washington will be upbeat and positive. In fact, government economists who even dare to suggest that the federal budget is out of control usually find themselves buried in the inner sanctum of Washington, or teaching Economics 101 at a community college somewhere.

I realize that I sound like a skeptic, and I openly admit that I am. But to be fair there are some honest politicians who have attempted to expose the truth and will continue to do so. Just look for those labeled "anti-progressive" and listen to them. If you would like a current list of those considered to be the most fiscally sound thinkers, you can write to The National Taxpayers' Union, 325 Pennsylvania Avenue, S.E., Washington D.C. 20003.

It is easy enough to find fault with a system like our federal bureaucracy because the abuses are visible for all to see. The question all Americans have to ask is, "What can be done about it?"

If there is nothing that can be done to change the situation, then all I will accomplish through this book is to depress some, disturb some others, and stir up a temporary flurry of activity.

I believe there is a great deal that can be done if God's people will wake up *now*. But if you get duped by the very voices I have warned against, they will convince you that this book, and all others like it, are just the distorted view of an alarmist, meant to promote some hidden agenda. This I promise you! I have no agenda other than to alert God's people to the looming crisis.

I absolutely believe what I have tried to convey to you. Obviously that does not necessarily mean I am correct; you'll have to evaluate that for yourself. But the statistics presented are easily verifiable. I have provided the sources in Appendix B. I encourage any skeptic to do the research necessary to satisfy yourself. If that doesn't convince you, then you cannot be convinced.

Perhaps some of my regular Christian readers are thinking, *Where does God fit into all this? Aren't we to trust in His provision?* Absolutely. Some of you may have been wondering why I used so few references to the only written source of absolute wisdom—God's Word—thus far. That was not an oversight. It was a deliberate decision on my part.

The information I have presented is both historical data and my personal interpretation of future events. I am not a prophet of God (that I am aware of). I have a real concern that those reading this book not link an economic forecast with scriptural doctrine. Obviously God is in control of our economy. This nation has been blessed because we have traditionally taken a strong stand for the Lord. Whether or not God will continue to bless us in the future, only He knows. Our responsibility is to obey for the sake of obedience—not profit.

Just as I believe our material wealth is a by-product of observing God's commandments and following His directions, so I believe the present state of our economy is an indication of violating basic biblical principles provided in the Bible.

In Deuteronomy 28:12-13 God makes His people a promise: "The Lord will open for you His good storehouse, the heavens, to give rain to your land in its season and to bless all the work of your hand; and you shall lend to many nations, but you shall not borrow. And the Lord shall make you the head and not the tail, and you only shall be above, and you shall not be underneath, if you will listen to the commandments of the Lord your God, which I charge you today, to observe them carefully."

Then in Deuteronomy 28:43-45 another sobering promise is made: "The alien who is among you shall rise above you higher and higher, but you shall go down lower and lower. He shall lend to you, but you shall not lend to him; he shall be the head, and you shall be the tail. So all these curses shall come on you and pursue you and overtake you until you are destroyed, because you would not obey the Lord your God by keeping His commandments and His statutes which He commanded you."

Take an objective look at our economy today and see for yourself if these passages describe where we are. I pray that we can turn this economy around and save our children and grandchildren from the scourges of depression and hyperinflation. If we can, there is no time to waste.

I have included the next chapter, a fictionalized account of an economic depression, to give you a perspective of what *could* be. It is a product of my imagination, based on the mounting evidence that an economic crisis is coming. This seemed the best way to convey what I am "feeling" without sounding "prophetic."

In chapter 15 I will return to reality and discuss what we can do to avert such a catastrophe.

The year is 1999. The president of the United States faces the greatest challenge the country has ever known . . .

14
The Economy in Crisis

The following is a *fictionalized* representation of what I visualize a collapse of the U.S. economy *could* be like. **All the names and events are totally fictitious.**

Jack Walton awoke on the morning of March 3, 1999, with a nagging feeling of dread inside. Events were taking place so rapidly that he could scarcely comprehend them.

First the Japanese had announced that they were suspending all further loans to the United States in retaliation for the trade restrictions the U.S. Congress had recently imposed.

Initially Jack had thought the congressional action was good; and it certainly was justified. The Congress had imposed a 50 percent tariff on all Japanese-made products where the same U.S. products were taxed in Japan. "After all, with only GM left in the car business, it certainly isn't fair for the Japanese to sell their cars in our country while our cars are priced out of the market in Japan," he told his wife Kathy.

The Nikkei index plummeted thirty thousand points in response to the imposed tariffs, and the Japanese retaliated swiftly, doubling the tariffs of goods made in the U.S. and sold in

Japan. They also ceased all loans to the U.S. and pressured the European community and the World Bank to join them in cutting off U.S. credit.

Ted Hacker, senator from Massachusetts, reacted by sponsoring a bill imposing even tighter restrictions on all Japanese sales. His new bill would place tariffs on goods manufactured in Japanese-owned plants in the U.S. in addition to the tariffs on imported goods.

Tensions escalated as the Japanese threatened to withdraw all their manufacturing from the U.S. if the bill was passed into law. The commerce department calculated that the closing of the Japanese-owned plants would idle an additional three million American workers. The situation had become one of economic brinkmanship, with American jobs being the pawns offered on the board.

Companies, pension plans, and millions of shareholders were wiped out.

Jack Walton was senior vice president at one of the Japanese-owned IBM computer facilities in Milwaukee. He knew that his plant would be one of the first to go in any economic shoving match. The Japanese could supply the same products from similar facilities in Poland and Russia. Jack had already heard rumblings about shifting some production to those facilities because of reduced labor costs. If the Japanese shut down only their IBM plants, it would idle nearly 800,000 American workers.

What in the world would I do? Jack thought as he lay in bed. *I'm fifty-four, and there's no place else I could go. How did we allow ourselves to get into this mess anyway?*

"Jack, are you OK?" Kathy Walton asked her husband. She was more worried about him than she was about what was happening in the economy. She knew from watching the news that emotions were running high between the Japanese and American governments. Jack was caught right in the middle of a power struggle between his country and Japan.

"I'm all right, honey," he said without any real conviction in his voice. "It's just hard to imagine what we're going to do if the Japanese close the plant. The economy is getting really bad."

"Surely they wouldn't just walk away from a plant worth millions of dollars . . . would they?" she asked. She had been trying to sort out what was happening herself. Jack had been so depressed she was afraid to talk with him about it. It seemed to her as if the whole economy just took a plunge when Bank of America failed.

In reality it had. The stock market dropped 900 points in one day—the largest single drop in the history of Wall Street, the analysts said. When the market recovered nearly 400 points the next week, most analysts assumed the economy would absorb the shock and continue on. They were totally wrong!

One week after the brief upswing, the market dropped another 1,000 points, and panic prevailed. At that point even the big mutual funds started dumping American stocks and shifting over to European and Asian market stocks to preserve their assets. Within a week the stock market had lost nearly *$3 trillion* in equity. Companies, pension plans, and millions of shareholders were wiped out.

When Jack heard Kathy's question, he knew she was trying to raise his spirits some. He thought, *I hate what's happening to me. I'm acting like an infant. I'm barely able to keep from crying.* Inside Jack knew his panic level was building.

Thinking back to the many orientation sessions he had attended after the Japanese bought the plant, he blurted out, "Those idiot politicians! Can't they see what they're doing? The Japanese are prideful people. To them, saving face is more important than profits. Our government is doing everything wrong. The Japanese will pull out. I know it!

"Look at what's happening. Nearly twelve million Americans are out of work already. What if this depression really does go five years? There won't be a building left standing in Milwaukee or any other city in America. Martial law in Milwaukee, Wisconsin! I would never have believed it possible. New York or Los Angeles, maybe, but not Milwaukee."

In Atlanta a meeting of the Federal Reserve Board was just starting. Paul Ott, the recently appointed chairman, was addressing the other board members, representing the regional reserve banks.

"Ladies and gentlemen, we now face the biggest crisis in our economy since 1929. The government's shortfall is running nearly $10 billion a day now, and virtually all outside loans have been cut off. The government will run out of operating funds at three o'clock today."

"What are the chances of funding another temporary bond issue?" Linda Worley, representative from Citicorp asked.

All of those present knew the answer. With the nation in the early stages of a deepening depression, there were not enough surplus funds available to feed the government's need.

"Not real good," Secretary of the Treasury Robert Dean replied. "We offered $20 billion yesterday at 18 percent, and more than half went unfunded. We monetized the rest to keep the whole bond market from collapsing."

The nation was a tinderbox just waiting to ignite.

That comment shocked the normally stoic bankers who let out an involuntary gasp.

"You mean you didn't actually sell out the issue yesterday?" Linda Worley asked in disbelief.

"No, but that information is to stay in this room! If word leaks out, there will be a panic in the market that will make the last downturn look like a bull market," Dean said sternly.

"How can we do that?" one of the other board members asked nervously. "That's illegal. We can't deceive people into thinking the debt has been funded when it hasn't. Monetizing that issue is tantamount to fraud."

"That is a noble sentiment," the treasury secretary commented caustically. "But the only other alternative is to shut down the government. Would any of you feel safe driving your car through the streets of your cities if we did that?"

"There is another alternative," Paul Brewster from Bankcorp retorted. "The Congress could actually decide to cut out about half of its spending and bring the deficits in line with income."

There was no further response from the treasury secretary. He knew, as they all did, that getting such a proposal through the Congress was impossible. *Besides, Dean thought, just the deficits created by the national health bill exceed the government's revenues by more than $600 billion a year, and next year the cost could be $3 trillion. Three trillion a year!* he thought with an involuntary shudder. *The liberals have wrecked our economy. The Health Care Bill was supposed to be limited to $100 billion a year—max.*

"What is the president's proposal, Mr. Secretary?" The chairman asked wearily. He knew, as they all did, that the nation was a tinderbox just waiting to ignite. One more bad report and the public just might panic. The president had already ordered the stock exchanges to place stop limits on all trades. Even with the down side limited, the market had dropped another 500 points.

"There is only one viable alternative," the secretary answered as he braced himself for the response he knew was sure to come. "The Treasury will print the money we need and funnel it out through the member banks. You'll have to buy the treasury issues in fictitious names."

The clamor in the room of normally reserved bankers sounded like an class of children who had just been told summer vacations were canceled.

"You can't do that, Mr. Secretary," Brewster said sharply. "That is blatant fraud . . . even counterfeiting."

"I'm afraid we don't have any other choice," Dean answered in a condescending tone. "It's either print some money and buy some time or risk a total collapse of this economy. Are you willing to risk that?"

"Don't try to lay that guilt trip on us, Mr. Secretary," Brewster shouted angrily. "You politicians created this mess. Now you expect us to clean it up!"

"I don't expect you to do anything except what you're told," Dean replied as he straightened his tie. "If you don't, you'll be responsible not only for the shutdown of our economic system but perhaps the collapse of our government as well. The choices are not those I desire either, but they're all we have. I would suggest we stop the melodramatics and get down to business."

Linda Worley was also fuming. She didn't like the pompous Texan who thought he knew all there was to know about running the economy. She and several others on the board had warned Dean and the president that the country was on a collision course with disaster the way they were spending money they didn't have.

She had seen the deficits climb from the ridiculous to the sublime. Now the monthly deficits were more than the annual deficits were five years earlier. And yet the politicians kept on spending—all the while insisting that the deficits didn't really matter.

She was about to give Dean a taste of her less-than-ladylike vocabulary when the chairman spoke up. "Please, let's stop this bickering among ourselves. The nation needs strong leadership now, not infighting.

"The policy committee met this morning and has already approved the temporary issuing of alternative currency."

Linda Worley's face dropped noticeably when she heard the chairman's announcement. *They knew about this yesterday,* she told herself. *It's already a fact. This meeting is just a formality,* she thought grimly as the truth hit her. *They funded the debt yesterday with fiat money to force the rest of us to comply.*

Three days later at the Northern Mutual Insurance Company in Omaha, Nebraska, the nation's fifth largest insurer, the president, Tom Henry, was worried.

"If we have another week like the last one we'll be in trouble, Ben," he told his comptroller. "Losses from the health side are crippling us, and policyholders are nervous since the article came out in *Money News* that our reserves are running low. With twelve smaller companies folding last week, it wouldn't take much to stampede them. Have you been able to arrange another line of credit?"

"Yes, sir," the thoroughly professional money manager replied. "Bankcorp promised us another $100 million against the policy reserves."

"Well, that's something at least," Henry replied as he slumped into his worn leather chair. "I hope we're not trading a short-term problem for a long-term one, though. If we strip all the reserves, we'll have a long road to recovery when the economy turns again."

"Yes, sir," Ben Parks agreed. It bothered him that they were pledging their best assets to cover withdrawals, but he could see no other choice either. If the policyholders couldn't recover their money as promised, the whole industry could be in trouble.

A thousand frantic policyholders jammed the phone lines demanding their money immediately.

Parks had tried to arrange a loan through two of the biggest secondary insurers, but even they didn't have the available cash. The treasury bond sales had stripped most of the available cash from the market. His boss, Tom Henry, had even made an attempt to secure a loan guarantee from the government similar to what Iacocca had done for Chrysler in the seventies, but to no avail. He didn't know the actual dialogue with the treasury secretary, but he knew the result—no money from the government.

When nine o'clock came around that Monday, their worst fears became a reality. The Sunday evening program, "Insider," had focused on the financial problems at Northern Mutual. And although their financial problems were not any worse than a dozen other similar companies, the interviewer had made it sound like the industry in general, and Northern Mutual in particular, was about to collapse.

"That may become a self-fulfilling prophecy," Tom Henry had commented to his wife, Nancy, as he had watched the program.

The interviewer had spread Mutual's financial troubles across the screen for all to see. The producers had even interviewed an elderly Northern Mutual policyholder who said she had been turned away Friday when she asked for her money.

What the producers didn't tell their viewers was that she had arrived ten minutes after the close of business hours. But the effect was dramatic. The cameras caught her clutching her old patent leather purse; tears were streaming down her wrinkled face.

"It's not fair, Tom," Nancy said angrily. "It's just a bunch of lies. The government passed laws requiring every insurance company to offer health insurance and then prohibited them from screening out bad risks, like the AIDS patients. It's not fair."

Tom Henry knew all too well that his wife was right, but there was nothing they could do about it. Ted Hacker and the other liberal spenders in the Congress had shifted their irresponsible policies over to the insurance companies. It was either write the health insurance or stop selling insurance altogether.

Maybe we would have served our policyholders better by stopping and distributing the cash we had then, he thought somberly. *Unless we can weather this panic for the next few days there won't be enough money to pay most of them a dime.*

The effect of the Sunday news program was evident as soon as the office opened that Monday. A thousand frantic policyholders jammed the phone lines demanding their money immediately.

Tom Henry knew he was out of options.

Outside the offices of Northern Mutual the lines had started forming even before business hours. When the doors were opened hundreds of local policyholders, who had seen the company through good times and bad in the past, rushed in to demand their money. By ten o'clock the meager reserves kept in the California bank used by the behemoth insurance company were depleted.

Ben Parks issued a wire transfer order from the recently established Bankcorp account to the First National Bank of Los

Angeles for $50 million. Five minutes later he received a fax that shook him to the core. He rushed into Tom Henry's office. "Mr. Henry, Bankcorp has reneged on their commitment. They won't release any funds."

"Why not?" Henry shouted at his ashen-faced comptroller.

"They say the run on Northern Mutual's reserves would put their funds in jeopardy, sir."

"That's nonsense!" Henry bellowed like a caged wild bull. "We have ten times in reserves what they're committing in cash. But we need that money to ride out this run; otherwise the whole company is in danger."

Tom Henry spent the next hour shouting over the phone at various employees of Bankcorp. But it was to no avail. He knew when he was being stonewalled. Bankcorp's directors were panicked too and didn't intend to be dragged down if Northern Mutual went under. Henry knew he would have no chance of arranging another line of credit now. Once the word got out, the bankers would treat him like a leper. *It's every man for himself now*, he thought angrily.

He made a one last call to the White House to see if he could get the president's help. He knew there was a great deal more at stake than just his company.

"This could be the start of an avalanche that can destroy the whole insurance industry," he told the president's economic adviser, Hal Downer. "And if the industry goes down, it'll drag the banks down with it."

Downer told him politely that he would pass the message along to the president but that he was in conference all afternoon and wouldn't be able to talk with him until the next day.

Wants to see if I'm still around tomorrow, Henry thought. "Thanks a lot, Mr. President," he said mockingly to the dead phone in his hand. "By tomorrow I'll be your worst nightmare, I suspect." With that he reached down and untied his wing tip shoes, trying to formulate his next plan of action.

Tom Henry knew he was out of options. He also knew he dreaded the next move even as he placed a call to Ron Whittaker, president of the First National Bank of Los Angeles.

Whittaker had been nervously awaiting the transfer of cash from Bankcorp. The overdrafts he had authorized for Northern Mutual were up to $42 million by the start of that day. *The money should have already been here,* he told himself fretfully.

He was shaking like a leaf when he answered the call from Tom Henry. "Tom, what's happening? You're having a heavy run on your accounts. Where's the money from Bankcorp?" Whittaker asked, his voice wavering from the panic he was feeling.

"It fell through, Ron. I guess it's that old 'dog-eat-dog' instinct coming out. I'm really sorry to put you in the middle of all this, but there's nothing I can do now."

"We'll be wiped out," the pudgy banker literally screamed as he pressed the phone tighter to his ear. "The lines are already forming here, and it's still an hour before we open."

"I know, Ron," Tom Henry said wearily. "It's no consolation, but at least our demise won't be as drawn out as some of the others. We're just the first of many casualties that will occur in this crash."

The newspapers and the evening newscasts all carried similar headlines: "Nation's Fifth Largest Insurer Collapses," "First National Bank of Los Angeles Fails," and "Nation's Banking System in Trouble."

The demise of Northern Mutual left nearly $20 billion in unfunded policies outstanding. Within two days three more California banks holding loans to First National filed for bankruptcy protection. Congress demanded that the president create a special fund to protect depositors' policyholders, but the White House refused to budge on its position that no more federal funds would be used to underwrite failing institutions. The FDIC was unable to cover any further depositors' losses.

Only the insiders knew that the government was having its own problems trying to stay afloat financially.

In the next three weeks, seven states declared their insolvency, defaulting on their bond payments to creditors. Nineteen states stopped or greatly curtailed their welfare programs, and virtually all the states reduced their staff to the survival level. Clearly the economy was coming apart at the seams, and no one seemed to have a clear picture of how to halt the process.

In the oval office at the White House, Treasury Secretary Robert Dean was addressing the president and his chief economic advisors.

"Mr. President, we're underfunded by nearly $30 billion a day. We'll need to increase the 'boost' to the money supply."

"This 'boost' you keep referring to is nothing more than counterfeiting currency," Andrew McMillan, the head of the senate banking committee, said disgustedly.

"It is a necessary enhancement to the system right now," Dean replied calmly. He knew the senate banking committee was dragging its feet, but they didn't have a better plan than the one he had proposed, so they would ultimately go along.

"Calm down Andrew," the president said. "None of us like this, but we can't just let the whole system grind to a halt. We have already agreed that boosting the money supply is the only choice available right now.

"Then why don't you go directly to the public and tell them the truth, Mr. President?" the senator from Ohio said angrily.

He had agreed to the money supply "enhancement" only as a temporary measure until a more permanent solution could be arranged. Now they were treating this counterfeiting as though it was a constitutional right.

The president knew that . . . the first time the money ran out, the U.S. economy would collapse totally.

"You know we can't do that, senator," the lanky treasury secretary from Texas said in his most exaggerated Southern drawl (meant to irritate the Northern senator), "If word of us printing money gets out, we'll have a real mess on our hands."

"Listen," Senator McMillan said sharply, directing his comments solely to the president. "The world bankers aren't stupid. They know what we're doing. Several of them have sent me only slightly veiled threats that they will look the other way for a short while only. If they sense we're stepping up the program they'll blow the whistle."

"What do you think, Robert?" the president asked of his treasury secretary.

"I don't think they will do anything, sir." They need us more than we need them. If they don't support the dollar, half the world will go broke," Dean said with a smug look on his face as he glanced over at the fuming senator.

Dean delighted in twisting the tail of his long-time opponent from Ohio. He had only accepted the appointment to the Treasury because he knew he would be able to influence monetary policy more as a cabinet member than he had as a minority member of the banking committee.

"The World Bank may be controlled by the European Community now, but they're not ready for a showdown with the United States."

That idiot, McMillan said silently. *He is so pompous he thinks the whole world dances to his music.* He thought about telling Dean so again, but decided there was nothing to be gained and knew there was too much at stake to start a feud. So he said as calmly as his elevated blood pressure would allow, "Mr. President, I disagree. The E.C. has already put a lot of its influence behind the Eurodollar. I believe they will offer a swap for U.S. dollars if they are forced to."

"Nonsense," Dean said in an obviously demeaning tone. "Sir, I respect my esteemed colleague from Ohio, but I think he is just running scared. Why that Eurodollar won't replace the U.S. dollar. Shoot! Nobody would trust it."

The president knew that half of what his Treasury chief said was just to irritate McMillan, but he also knew that the first time the money ran out, the U.S. economy would collapse totally; his advisers had made that painfully clear with their predictions of anarchy in the streets.

In the end he realized he had no other choice. The American people were not mentally equipped to face a prolonged depression, and that was the only alternative he could see.

On July 14, 1999, the Japanese made good their threat to shut down their manufacturing facilities in the U.S. Two days earlier Congress had overridden the president's veto of the internal Tariff Act, levying a 50 percent excise tax on all goods in the U.S. by foreign-owned companies.

The president appealed to the Japanese leaders to wait until the Supreme Court had a chance to review the issue before reacting. He was certain the high court would rule the Tariff Act unconstitutional.

The Japanese were not in a negotiating mood since the militants in Japan were demanding immediate retaliation. The Japanese leaders had presumed the Congress would back down rather than risk an additional three million Americans losing their jobs. They were sure they would once the plants started closing.

Instead, the Congress assumed the posture of a government at war and, in a further escalation of the trade war, immediately voted to freeze all foreign investors' assets in American companies.

The ranks of the unemployed swelled each week as more businesses were closed and others failed as a result. Even those whose products were sold primarily inside the country were suffering because of the scarcity of parts normally provided by foreign companies. Americans quickly discovered that nearly 70 percent of all businesses were dependent either upon foreign sales or supplies. Within two months of the Tariff Act's implementation, the unemployed ranks swelled to nearly 18 percent of all workers.

The choices were out of the president's control. It was either print more money or risk anarchy.

For the first time in more than fifty years, Americans saw the specter of millions of homeless people out of work and out of hope. Lines formed outside every government welfare agency; inside, token crews of paid staff and volunteers had to tell those who applied that there were no funds available for unemployment or welfare.

State revenues dropped by nearly 40 percent as millions of families lost their homes and jobs and hundreds of banks failed.

All but the most essential governmental services, such as police, prisons, and fire fighting were suspended or reduced greatly.

The nightly newscasts were like scenes from a science fiction movie with arsonists' fires lighting up the skyline of the major cities. The reduced police forces were delegated to arresting arsonists and looters. Minor crimes like burglary and purse snatching simply went uninvestigated.

To most Americans, the economy was a nightmare from which they expected to awaken at any moment. But September 21, 1999, would be remembered as the day the economy suffered its worst blow.

The European Community directors had been meeting for several days, trying to formulate a policy for how to handle the U.S. currency problem. The Asian Triangle, consisting of Japan, Korea, and China had been pressuring the E.C. to devalue the dollar, based on the estimates of its dilution provided by the World Bank.

The figures showed that nearly $1 trillion had been printed since early July, with twice that amount needed to fund the U.S. debt through the end of the current year. Even a third-year graduate student knew the dollar had been badly inflated and should be devalued. But deciding on the disciplinary measures had been difficult with Britain supporting its long-time friend and ally.

As the uncontrolled printing of money continued, it became obvious to all that the U.S. was not going to be able to bring its deficits under control. Even a personal appeal by the British prime minister had not been able to persuade the American president to stop inflating the dollar.

In actuality, the choices were out of the president's control. It was either print more money or risk anarchy.

On September 21 the E.C., in coordination with the World Bank, devalued the U.S. dollar by 60 percent; even that was a compromise demanded by the British member of the council.

Once the word was made public, investors outside the U.S. rushed to convert their U.S. dollars into the E.C. Eurodollar, adopted as the official world currency by virtually all members of the World Economic Council, excluding the United States of course.

In one swift move, the U.S. dollar was cut loose from all supports and allowed to sink or rise, based on its perceived value.

Inside the United States, panic dominated the dwindling banking community as foreign lenders demanded that their dollars be converted to the new world currency. Banks that had survived the economic crisis by drawing upon loans from long-time foreign investors found themselves cut off from any future source of funds unless they complied—which they did.

Overnight the dollar dropped to one-tenth of its previous value on the world market; America was bankrupt.

Inside the U.S. those who had any cash converted it into anything they could buy, from antique art to land. But as the sellers discovered they had traded real assets for rapidly deflating currency, they raised their prices—often as much as 100 percent per day!

Americans flocked to the stores to buy whatever was available before the prices went up further. This increased demand simply drove the prices of available merchandise out of the reach of all but those with abundant supplies of money.

The price of a loaf of bread that sold for $1.80 a week before the devaluation soared to over $60 and continued to inflate 10 percent daily. Gasoline sold for $20 a gallon, when it could be purchased at all. Virtually all imports from the Arab oil producers had been diverted to countries that paid in Eurodollars.

Homeowners, businesses, and college students saw their debts double, triple, and quadruple monthly.

Crime became so rampant in the major cities throughout the country that the National Guard was called out to patrol the streets after the federally mandated ten o'clock curfew. It was clear that American society was coming apart.

In one of those all too frequent tragedies, Jack Walton, the former vice president of IBM in Milwaukee, committed suicide in his despondency over losing his career. He left a note telling his wife Kathy that his insurance would provide adequately for her and the children. What Jack didn't know was that his insurer, American Casualty, would succumb to the increasing mortality in the insurance industry. Kathy Walton read about the company's bankruptcy less than a week after Jack's death.

The more the U.S. dollar was devalued, the more money that was needed. Hundred dollar bills became the smallest denomination printed, for the sake of cost. By November a hundred dollar bill would no longer buy a hamburger at a fast food restaurant. The standard currency became items of barter such as jewelry, gold, or individual state vouchers, which were often more dependable than the dollar.

In an unprecedented move, the Congress passed legislation indexing all mortgages to the devaluation of the dollar, retroactive to September when the inflation began. Homeowners, businesses, and college students saw their debts double, triple, and quadruple monthly in a futile effort to help salvage the remaining lenders. Millions of families filed for bankruptcy protection as the lenders repossessed homes, cars, and even furniture.

In the office of the president, a crisis meeting was taking place with the leaders of the Senate and House, as well as several leading national businessmen representing the newly formed group, the Business Coalition for a Stable Economy (BCSE).

Joseph Wallace, president of the BCSE addressed his longtime friend. "Mr. President, I don't see what choice we have. If this cycle continues, the dollar will go the way of the German reichmark. It has already dropped by 500 percent in the last month. Another couple of months of this and it will be totally worthless."

"The BCSE will support your decision to adopt the Eurodollar as our official currency. We have the promise of the E.C. that if the U.S. drops the sanctions and frees the foreign deposits they will accept the swap at $500 per Euro."

"That's outright theft," Senator McMillan said angrily. "Sure, those with millions will do okay, but what about those who lost their life savings as a result of our government's madness?"

"It's either that or risk burning the country to the ground, Senator," Robert Dean said with the slightest sign of a smirk showing on his face.

"You were the one who was so sure you could stabilize the currency," McMillan spat out, glaring at the man he had come to despise so thoroughly. "Now you want to make the United States a lackey of the Europeans. How much are they paying you?"

"Why you arrogant idiot!" Dean growled through clenched teeth. "If you and your cronies hadn't spent the country into poverty with your give-away programs, we wouldn't be in this mess in the first place!"

"That's enough!" the president said sternly. "It doesn't matter how or why we got here; here we are. Now I want to discuss the best course to follow in what we all agree is a bad situation."

"I say we don't have a choice," Paul Ott, the Federal Reserve chairman, said matter-of-factly. "If we don't adopt their rules and exchange our currency, the dollar will be totally worthless by the first quarter of next year. We can either spend the next ten years in a depression or face the hard decisions right now."

"What about this requirement that we adopt a cash-less system when we convert?" the president asked his Treasury secretary.

The move to the cash-less system was hailed by both merchants and media.

The president had just sat through two hours of grilling by the leaders of the evangelical council who argued against any such move. *Or more correctly, railed against it,* he thought. They had accused him of everything from treason to being the antichrist.

"We have to do it," Dean said. "It will shut down the crime in the cities and will make the transition to the Eurodollar much

faster. Besides, practically no one uses currency anymore anyway."

With life in America rapidly degrading to a subsistence level for most families, and with violence escalating rapidly, those
in the room knew there were no other choices left.

*The choices should have been made back in the seventies,
or eighties,* the president thought morosely. *I should have made
them myself when I came into office. Now all we have left are
some very bad alternatives. There is no doubt that our country
has become the lenders' slave.*

"I agree," the president said as he signed the currency bill
authorizing the Treasury to accept the Eurodollar exchange.
With that done, he also signed the authorization to convert to
the non-currency system known as "Data-Net."

Once the currency exchange bill was passed, the changes
came swiftly. One week was allowed for all existing U.S. currency to be exchanged for Eurodollars or, more correctly, Eurocre-
dits. These credits could then be used to purchase needed
supplies at the federally established prices. No other currency
would be honored.

All transactions would be processed through the centralized Federal Reserve system known as Data-Net via computer-
ized cash registers in each store. In one week, the U.S. dollar
that had survived the Civil War, two world wars, and several
previous depressions, was gone. The move to the cash-less system was hailed by both merchants and media as a decisive and
innovative step in halting the crime spree in the cities.

All foreign assets were unfrozen as a part of the agreement
with the E.C. The majority of these assets were reinvested in the
depressed U.S. economy. Closed plants began to reopen with
more than 70 percent of all businesses under foreign ownership.

Most Americans found themselves strapped for any funds
beyond those necessary for the most basic needs. With federal
welfare funds all but eliminated and most savings gone, the majority of retirees were forced back into the job market.

The economy remained stuck in a depression of unprecedented magnitude with more than 15 percent of all Americans
still unemployed or underemployed. The currency bill had
stopped the plummet into the abyss, but it would be many years

before American consumers recovered any significant buying power. In the meantime, most of the goods manufactured in the U.S. were exported to the richer developing nations in Europe, with the majority of the profits returning to foreign investors. America had become a colony once more.

Six months later in the Houston offices of Robert Dean, former secretary of the Treasury, a call came in from the administrative director of the World Bank.

"We all want to thank you for your help in resolving a most difficult situation, Mr. Dean," the director said, "I assure you that we will place a great deal of business with your law firm in the future."

"Thank you," Dean responded with gusto in his voice, belying his age of nearly seventy. Dean prided himself on the fact that often people thought him to be twenty years younger. "Everything went just as you predicted. Once the economy crumbled the liberals had no choice but to join. When do you plan the next phase?"

"We will begin implementing the cash-less system worldwide in less than a year. With your country already adapting to the system, I believe there will be little opposition. Soon every transaction in the world will be recorded and monitored instantaneously. We will be well on the way to the one-world system we have dreamed about for so long."

"I look forward to working with you," Dean said. "It is time the people of this world stop thinking nationally and begin to think globally. I believe in twenty years we will be able to eliminate world hunger—perhaps even poverty."

"Yes. . ." the other man agreed as he nodded his head. But he knew that was not the agenda his "Society" had in mind. *Let them think what they want,* he muttered softly as he hung up the phone and turned back to his desk. *Poverty serves our needs for cheap labor. . .*

Please bear in mind that what you have read here is a *fictionalized* representation of what an economic collapse *could* do. We can avoid this and other similar scenarios if we decide to do something *now!* The next chapter is dedicated to what can be done.

It would be easy to assume that it is someone else's responsibility to correct the problems or to assume that the politicians will suddenly wake up and do what's right. Unfortunately, neither is true. Unless the American people demand responsible economics from their elected officials, this economy will go the way of all previous economies: into oblivion.

It is important that citizens get involved in the federal budget process. The best way to do this is by combining forces with one of the "watch dog" groups in Washington and holding the politicians accountable for their decisions.

The threat of last resort is a constitutional amendment that will force the budget to be brought into balance. The critical question is: Are Americans willing to pay the price to save our economy?

15
What Can You Do?

As I have been writing this book I've been thinking about what advice to give the readers. The quandary I always have with giving advice is whether or not I'm willing to accept my own advice and actually do something different as a result. In all honesty, I have to admit that as I've reread this work myself I have been startled by some of the statistics presented. What you are reading is a condensed version of a large volume of statistics my researcher and I have accumulated over a long period of time. When I saw them all in one place I wasn't prepared for the impact it had on me. We are headed for an economic earthquake disaster of unparalleled magnitude, and it is difficult to see anything that can be done to avert it at this time.

The one certainty is that God is still in control no matter what happens. I continually remind myself that the Lord said not even a sparrow falls to the ground without His knowledge. That really is comforting, even if you happen to be that sparrow.

However, knowing that God is in control does not remove our responsibility to do everything possible to change what is happening or to prepare ourselves for some difficult times. As

Proverbs 16:9 says, "The mind of man plans his way, but the Lord directs his steps."

The theme of a popular song a few years ago was "I didn't promise you a rose garden." The same theme can be applied to God's people in this world. Perhaps it is His will that we suffer some hard times. There is nothing that will bring the saved or unsaved to their knees like seeing their economic foundations shattered.

Most Christians in America are as much a part of the problem as anyone else.

I truly believe the decade ahead of us will provide the greatest opportunity to witness of any since the first century. We have the means to reach everyone who will listen through the electronic media; we have the trained people who can touch every level of society; and we will have the opportunity when the whole world seems to be in chaos.

The logical question that needs to be asked is, "Will Christians be a part of the solution . . . or a part of the problem?" As of this minute I would say that most Christians in America are as much a part of the problem as anyone else. There is basically no difference in how the average Christian handles his or her finances compared to the average non-Christian.

Too often Christians think that because they *are* Christians God is obligated to keep them from all harm. There are two basic flaws in that mentality.

First, a great many Christians are violating basic biblical principles in the areas of personal and business finances. God is under no obligation to bail them out of situations He has specifically warned them against in the first place. That doesn't mean that He won't. God is long-suffering when it comes to our disobedience. But it may also mean that when the Scripture gives us ample warnings we are to obey or suffer the consequences. As Proverbs 1:32-33 says, "For the waywardness of the naive shall kill them, and the complacency of fools shall destroy them.

But he who listens to me shall live securely, and shall be at ease from the dread of evil."

Second, it may well be God's plan to allow His people, or at least some of them, to suffer along with the unbelievers. We are to witness to those around us that God is sufficient in *all* things. If Christians were removed from every problem that befalls this society, we certainly would attract a large following, but for the wrong reasons. God desires followers who will serve Him regardless of the costs. Adversity seems to strengthen us, whereas prosperity tends to weaken us. As the prophet said in Proverbs 30:8-9, "Keep deception and lies far from me, give me neither poverty nor riches; feed me with the food that is my portion, lest I be full and deny Thee and say, 'Who is the Lord?' or lest I be in want and steal, and profane the name of my God."

The temptations in poverty are more black and white than they are in riches. In poverty the choice is usually between being honest or dishonest. In riches we can drift away from God without even realizing it.

God will often allow His disciples (followers) to suffer adversity for the benefit of His work. You need only look to the lives of His own apostles to verify this.

What it really boils down to is this:

1. Many Christians will suffer needlessly because of their own foolish decisions and failure to plan properly, based on God's Word.
2. Others will suffer through no fault of their own simply because God wants to use them as examples of steadfastness in the face of adversity.
3. There will be some Christians who will experience God's supernatural provision—mentally, financially, physically, and spiritually.

If I have a choice, I'll choose the last group, thank you very much. But since the choice is God's, not ours, the best you and I can do is ensure that we don't inhibit God's help because of our own foolish decisions.

Psalm 50, verses 14 and 15 are some of my most cherished Scriptures. "Offer to God a sacrifice of thanksgiving, and pay your vows to the Most High; and call upon Me in the day of trouble; I shall rescue you, and you will honor Me."

In these passages we are given a marvelous promise: that God will come and rescue us in our "day of trouble." I have experienced this firsthand many times. It is wonderful to stand back and see God's provision when there seems to be no human way to resolve a situation. However, if you will read those verses carefully you will find that there are some prerequisites that must first be met.

The certainty is that without sacrifice there can be no rewards.

We are told in verse 14 to offer a sacrifice of "thanksgiving" to God. The term "sacrifice" means to surrender something we have our hearts set on (literally to give up a desire). For me at least, this has always meant the right to make my own decisions. Once I made the decision to invite Christ into my life, I gave up the right to make my own decisions. As long as I practice this principle diligently, the Lord can bless me. The instant I stop doing this, the Lord is constrained by His own Word from coming to my rescue.

Obviously there are many other areas of our lives that must be in compliance with God's Word also, but for me personally, this represents the greatest challenge. For others it may be surrendering the "perfect" home, or the right car, or giving up a retirement plan, or some other desire. The certainty is that without sacrifice there can be no rewards. That was true for Abraham, just as it is true for us today.

The second prerequisite for receiving God's help is to "pay our vows." A vow is a promise made to the Lord. Every person who has been saved into God's kingdom has made some fundamental vows that must be kept if God is to bless and protect them.

The apostle Paul said in Romans 10:9, "If you confess with your mouth Jesus as Lord, and believe in your heart that God raised Him from the dead, you shall be saved."

These are the two absolute vows made by *everyone* who has accepted Jesus Christ as Savior. The first is to confess Jesus as Lord. To confess Jesus as Lord with your mouth means to "agree" with God that His Son is our omnipotent authority. The term *omnipotent* means "absolute and without challenge."

If Christ is the total and absolute authority in our lives, we will obey His teachings. The Lord said in Luke 6:46, "Why do you call Me 'Lord, Lord,' and do not do what I say?" It cannot be said any clearer. If we call Christ Lord, we must also obey Him. The way we handle our finances is one of the clearest indicators of whether or not we are obedient to the Lord. In Matthew 7:21 Jesus said, "Not everyone who says to Me, 'Lord, Lord,' will enter the kingdom of heaven; but he who does the will of My Father who is in heaven."

Our second promise or vow is to "believe in our hearts" that Christ is risen from the dead. I don't know what this means to you, but to me it means that I must live my life in such a manner that Christ working through me can witness to others that He is still alive.

If my life (or yours) is lived in a manner that never reflects any supernatural circumstances, there is virtually no witness for Christ's resurrection.

There are many non-Christians who are nice, philanthropic people. Unfortunately many of them actually live a better lifestyle than many of those who claim to be Christians. But their lives reflect none of the supernatural that was so common in the Lord's day. They are basically nice people who help ease a lot of misery on this earth, but they do nothing to ease the greater misery the vast majority will suffer for eternity.

Our lives are to reflect something greater: Jesus Christ. If we do, He has committed Himself to our rescue because then *He* will receive the glory, not us. There is an old cliché that I like to use when describing God's rescue: "never late, rarely early."

I have offered this brief review of financial principles simply to emphasize what God's Word teaches: that God will intercede on our behalf if we will allow Him to. But we can block His help by our own stubborn disobedience and disregard of His Word.

Obviously anyone wants God's help in times of trial; often there is no other place to turn. But the time to secure His help in this coming economic earthquake is right now, through obedience to His teachings and personal leading.

Only the Lord knows the future, and only the Lord has control over the future. However, by observing His principles we can make our future a whole lot less vexing. God allows us to be a part of His decision-making process. His Word teaches that we are to be a part of His plan, not just an observer of it.

"The mind of man plans his way, but the Lord directs his steps" (Proverbs 16:9).

There are some things everyone can do to prepare for the economic earthquake that is coming. These do not include buying guns, gold, dehydrated foods, and a cabin in the north woods as some suggest. God did not raise up an army to have us cut and run every time things get rough.

The one nonvariable is this: what you own belongs to you and not a lender.

When times were difficult for the believers in Jerusalem, God had already planned for their needs through diligent converts who were debt-free and able to share with others (see Acts 4:34-35). Remember that by standing together we can meet every need and still have an abundance left over. But God's plan involves disciplined people who will read the signs and then act in accordance.

GET OUT OF DEBT

Recently I wrote a book entitled *Debt-Free Living*. In it I tried to discuss all the arguments for and against borrowing in our economy, so I won't expound on that material here. However, I believe there are some pertinent points that must be made in relation to the coming crisis in our economy.

First, debt created this problem, and debt will make it far worse before we see any resolution. Debt is not the problem though; debt is merely the mechanism by which weak-willed politicians feed their constituents easy money—which is what borrowed money is. Debt, therefore, has allowed the government to spend money it didn't have on projects that most Americans wouldn't have approved if they had been required to pay for them with tax dollars.

Second, there is no way to sustain debt spending for an indefinite period of time. Eventually the interest accumulation will exceed anyone's (or any country's) ability to keep the debt current.

Let me restate an absolute principle of economics: No one, government or otherwise, can spend more than he makes indefinitely. At some point the compounding interest will consume all the money in the world. We might disagree about *when* the end will come, but not *if*.

Compounding is the fatal flaw in every pyramid "get rich scheme," declared to be illegal by the very government that is promoting the biggest pyramid scheme in history.

I have often asked young college students this question: If you had the choice of taking a million dollars in cash or one penny that is doubled daily for thirty days, which would you choose? Invariably they choose the million in cash. And yet, the penny, working through the mechanism of compounding interest, would be worth approximately $300 million in thirty-five days.

The same mechanism is at work on our national debt. At a mere 8 percent per year interest, the debt will double every nine years, even if the annual deficits were eliminated today!

It certainly doesn't take a statistician to figure out that a $3 trillion debt in 1991 becomes $6 trillion in 2000 just from interest accumulation. Let me assure any skeptics that your wages won't double in the same time period—not unless prices quadruple.

With so many variables in the economy, the one nonvariable is this: What you *own* belongs to *you* and not a lender. There are many people who could be debt-free just by moving funds from one investment to another, such as withdrawing funds from a retirement account to pay off their home mortgage. The reason most don't is that someone has convinced them it makes more sense to pay the interest and save the taxes.

Many unfortunate people have discovered that what seems to make sense in a stable economy becomes nonsensical in a volatile economy. I have already demonstrated that paying interest makes no sense. Unless you're in a 101 percent tax bracket, you lose more interest than you gain in tax refund.

For those who are at least twenty years from retirement it makes economic sense to concentrate on debt retirement before saving for retirement. This is true even though the retirement funds are tax deferred, or even if the funds must be removed from an existing retirement plan.

Currently, if you take an early withdrawal on a retirement account, you will have to pay additional taxes and a penalty for early withdrawal (for those under the age of 59½). Even so, it still makes economic sense to take the penalty and pay the taxes just to know your home is debt-free. If you can't pay your real estate taxes in a bad economy, you can lose your home in three years (in most states). However, if you can't pay the mortgage payments you can lose it in three months.

You need to look at every loan you make from this point on to determine what the contingent liabilities are. If you are obligated beyond the assigned collateral, don't borrow! If you already have loans where you are in surety, do everything possible (within reason) to retire the outstanding loans and avoid any future surety.

It is in the interest of those who rent money to keep the majority of people borrowing.

For some people, it doesn't make good economic sense to sell assets or strip a retirement plan to pay off loans if they are forced to do so in a bad economy. But set as a goal to be debt-free as soon as possible. When the economy recovers, and it will, don't change your mind because things are looking better. Read the indicators and believe that our economy has some problems that cannot (or will not) be resolved.

If the economy fails before the end of this decade, there will be some people who cannot get totally debt-free. But if I am off by even 10 percent, and that's entirely possible, virtually anyone who desires to can get debt-free. There is no better time to begin than right now, and it starts with an attitude adjustment.

This adjustment is to make up your mind that God's Word governs your decisions, not someone else's idea of financial logic. It is in the interest of those who rent money to keep the majority of people borrowing. God's Word says that a wise man looks ahead to see if there is a problem coming and tries to avoid it. Only a naive person proceeds without caution (my paraphrase of Proverbs 27:12).

RETIREMENT PLANNING

At the risk of sounding radical, I'm going to suggest that if you are at least twenty years away from retirement you put aside your retirement goals for at least five years and concentrate on the more immediate needs, such as retiring your debts first. This may sound like a restatement of what I just discussed, and it is. But it makes economic as well as biblical sense to get totally out of debt before starting a retirement plan, especially looking ahead to some of the problems we are facing.

If you weigh the alternatives of either starting a retirement plan while paying off your home or using the retirement funds to pay your home off early and then starting the retirement plan, there is no contest. Assuming you have at least twenty years before retirement, you will do much better financially by paying the mortgage off first. It's the simple concept of compounding interest working for you rather than against you. For those who have never considered this, the following chart, borrowed from a previous book I wrote, will verify it for you.

The example I used was a thirty-five year old who plans to retire at age sixty-five. He can save $100 in a retirement account for thirty years while paying off his home mortgage ($100,000 at 10 percent), or he can use his extra $100 a month to prepay his mortgage and then start his retirement account.

Plan A shows him paying the mortgage while paying into the retirement account.

Plan B shows him paying off the mortgage, then starting the retirement account. The savings in the retirement account are compounded at 6 percent annually.

Plan A	Plan B
$100,000 mortgage at 10% for 30 yrs. = $315,918 $100 per month invested in retirement account at 6% for 30 yrs. = $101, 054 (approx.) NET RESULT: 1. Home paid off (age 65) 2. $101,054 in savings at age 65	$100,000 mortgage at 10% for 30 yrs. plus $100 per month additional principal payment. A savings of $90,104 is realized as home is paid off in 19.3 years. = $225,814 After home is paid off, equivalent payments (mortgage amount plus $100) are invested in a retirement account at 6% for 10.7 years. = $178,395 NET RESULT: 1. Home paid off (age 54) 2. $178,395 in savings at age 65

If you are within ten years of retirement, or are retired already, I would suggest some radical changes in your perspective.

For those with sizeable assets ($250,000 or more) I suggest that you follow Solomon's advice and diversify as rapidly as the economy will allow. "Divide your portion to seven, or even to eight, for you do not know what misfortune may occur on the earth" (Ecclesiastes 11:2).

You need to look at investing in some assets outside the United States through quality mutual funds and other instruments that have sound track records. The certainty is that the whole world's economy will not fail. Some countries will benefit while others will suffer. The difficulty is in determining which will benefit and which will not. The best "hedge" is to diversify as much as possible—not only in different areas of the economy, but also in different areas of the world. For instance, don't keep all of your assets in California real estate, even if it has always done well for you. We have not had a major economic tremor in the last fifty years, much less an earthquake.

If your assets are invested too narrowly, your risk is multiplied.

The one caution I would give is don't be panicked into making foolish investments by following the advice of those who profit from fear. More often than not these are the "gold bugs." They would have everyone place a large amount of their assets in gold or silver as protection against the big collapse.

I might put a lot more confidence in their suggestions if someone other than a gold salesman would substantiate their confidence in precious metals. There is no doubt that our economy would be better off today if we had remained on the gold standard. But we have been divorced from it for more than fifty years now. In my opinion, neither the United States nor any other major economic power will return to the gold standard in our lifetimes. To do so would require that gold be revalued to approximately $64,000 an ounce. It is far more likely that we will evolve into a totally cash-less economy as a result of the coming crisis, not one based on precious metals.

For those with lesser assets and less flexibility with their retirement assets I would suggest two things: First, seek some alternative vocational training during the interval between the next upswing in the economy and the earthquake that appears to be coming. Any investment can be lost, no matter how secure it appears at present. But vocational skills will last for as long as you live and will be marketable regardless of the economy.

It is important to understand that not everyone will be mired down economically in a depression (or even in hyperinflation). Many people will actually prosper during this period as they have the resources to take advantage of the opportunities presented. This group will have the assets to pay for the services they need. So take a course in plumbing, electricity, carpentry, cabinetmaking, computer science, or anything else that is marketable. Determine what your basic aptitudes are and exploit them to the highest degree possible. If you can become highly proficient at any one thing, you will rarely be without a source of income.

The second suggestion is to diversify even with limited assets. You may not be able to buy land in Poland or Yugoslavia, but you can invest in a good international mutual fund. If your assets are invested too narrowly, your risk is multiplied. Remember that the goal is not necessarily to maximize your return as much as it is to minimize your losses.

If you are retired, out of debt, and have some surplus money, in a deflationary economy your dollars will stretch farther. But if you're retired, living on a fixed income with limited assets and hit a hyperinflationary cycle, your life savings can be consumed in a startlingly short amount of time. So it is important not to get stuck in a no-risk mentality about investing. Treasury bonds may be great in a stable or deflationary economy because they are virtually risk free. But if you believe any of the suppositions I have presented on hyperinflation might come true, you would do well to place some of your retirement assets in investments such as growth mutual funds and international funds. They won't do well during a deflationary cycle, but they will keep pace with the economy in an inflationary period.

We have allowed the political process to create a new caste system.

What happens if the government decides to absorb your retirement funds into the Social Security system? Then you simply say that you have done the best you can with what you had and go back to work again. In the meantime I would not put all my surplus into a retirement account, even if I could. In the highest tax bracket you still pay only 33 percent of your earnings in federal income taxes (at present). The after-tax surplus can be invested in tax-deferred investments, such as annuities totally outside the retirement system. Based on the past actions of our government, I believe it is worth paying the taxes and controlling at least some of your savings.

One additional thing you can do is write and call your elected officials to get their official positions on the theft of funds from the Social Security Trust. If they won't take a public stand against this, make it a campaign issue during the next election. You would be amazed how agreeable many politicians are during an election period. The greatest asset we have as voters is public awareness.

GET INVOLVED

I am amazed how few people ever get involved in the political process. They have been brainwashed into believing that their voices don't really count; believe me they do.

I had a senator tell me that as few as two hundred calls or letters for or against a particular bill will often sway his vote. He also added that many of his colleagues have voiced the same comment.

> *We have surrendered control of our finances to a group of people ignorant in basic economics.*

We have allowed the political process to create a new caste system, with our elected officials serving like a collective monarchy. They pass laws restricting the rights and freedoms for the majority of Americans, while exempting themselves from the process.

I doubt that many voters know the Congress has exempted itself from all the civil rights and anti-discrimination laws passed. They have exempted themselves from our retirement system, our school system (for their own children), and even the normal day-care system.

It is a fact that those who vote to expand the rights of criminals and restrict the rights of the victims are themselves afraid to walk the streets of our nation's capital. The days when Harry

Truman could walk the streets with little more than a token force of secret service men are over. Today the president needs an armored car and a bullet-proof vest.

The same political system that allows taxpayers' funds to be spent for a study of why bees can fly ($378,000), free playing cards for Air Force II ($52,000), anti-Christian art ($480,000), and a congressional workout room ($42,000,000), also allows for our tax dollars to be poured down another ten thousand "rat holes."

Why should we think that our governmental leaders would suddenly get conservative when it comes to running our nation's economy? We have surrendered control of our finances to a group of people ignorant in basic economics. It is time that the average American woke up and realized that a housewife who has learned to live on an average income is imminently more qualified to make economic decisions than is the average politician.

This is not a philosophical or even a political issue. It is our future we're discussing, and if we don't make some dramatic changes, it is just a matter of time before the economy fails. Keep in mind that the people who are trying to convince us that an economic crisis will not occur are the same ones who spend $500 for hammers that are commercially available for $12, buy 20¢ bolts for $60, spend $40 billion a year in taxpayers' funds not to grow food, and increase the welfare rolls from 6 million to 14 million people while spending $3 trillion to accomplish this remarkable task.

The list of abuses could go on and on. The point is, the next time you think that you may not be qualified to counsel the politicians on how the economy should be run, consider whether or not you would pay annual bonuses to the post office administrators who operate the postal system in the red each and every year.

If you balance your checkbook every month you're probably better qualified economically than the majority of our budget directors. I have often believed that the nation's budget director should be required to demonstrate that he lives on a budget himself. But perhaps that's too simplistic for Washington.

If you don't want your children and grandchildren to live in a third-rate country with fewer jobs and total dependency on foreign goods and money, you *need* to get involved.

As Harry Figgie accurately stated, "This is not a Republican or a Democratic problem. It is an American problem."

I will admit that I am a radical when it comes to this issue. I watch the economy month in, month out, and I see the steady decline in productivity and competitiveness. I see politicians chiding the "wealthy" and then voting salaries for themselves that place them in the top 5 percent of incomes in America. I see honest small business people struggling to survive under the heavy burden of taxes, insurance, and foreign competition. Our political system makes us especially vulnerable to outside competition because our government gives benefits to our competitors while penalizing American companies. It would seem the basic philosophy of our government is help your enemies and hurt your friends. The Japanese, for instance, consider their entrepreneurs as a national resource and do everything possible to preserve and protect them—even creating special legislation in order to make them more competitive.

We do the exact opposite. President Calvin Coolidge once said, "The chief business of American people is business." Our present herd of politicians no longer accept that doctrine. Their philosophy is "The business of America is politics." Unfortunately they have been quite successful in convincing Americans that the economy runs to serve the political system.

This constant and growing drain on our resources strips the business community of the vital capital needed to create more jobs and compete with countries that take our innovations and sell them back to us.

Allow me to outline a few specific suggestions that you can use when contacting your senators and congressman.

1. Demand that the Congress and the president abide by the Gramm-Rudman Act and balance the national budget— immediately.

I would further demand that *all* spending programs be included in the law—no exceptions. Until and unless all spending is included "in-budget" the law will not work. It is very much like the wage and price controls we discussed earlier; the exceptions quickly become the norm.

What happens in the Washington political system is a process called "trade offs." In this process those who want something trade a favor for a favor. The result is usually legislation that is good for their district but bad for the country. The only way to avoid this (if at all) is to require all programs to be cut by the same percentage and to allow line-item vetoes so that so-called "pork barrel" spending is not attached to nonrelated legislation.

2. *Keep track of how the politicians in your area vote on spending bills.*

The group known as Citizens Against Government Waste (see Appendix A) watches this area carefully and publishes a quarterly report. I can assure you that if you come to an election meeting armed with specific facts about how your representatives voted to use taxpayers' money, they will think about the bills they back the next time they vote in Washington.

The number for the Citizens Against Government Waste is 1-800-USA-DEBT, and the address is 1301 Connecticut Avenue, N.W., Suite 400, Washington, D.C. 20036.

3. *Every chance you get, challenge the mentality that all business people and the profits they generate are somehow inherently evil. That is total nonsense and merely a method of "scapegoating."*

Instead, begin to prompt your elected officials to use the system to promote more competitive enterprises. I personally would like to see the government allow tax-free return on investments made to businesses that compete directly with foreign imports.

In reality we would be losing very few tax dollars since these are industries where we are no longer competitive anyway. And for every tax dollar lost, it has been shown that we would gain nearly $1,000 in taxable revenue.

Such an idea would not sit well with the liberals who point their fingers at the "greedy" businessmen, but it will sit very well with the Americans who find new jobs opening up.

It is a national disgrace that Americans invented the multi-valve car engine, video recorders, color television, digital electronics, computer-controlled machines, and so on, but are no longer competitive in any of these industries.

It is *not* that the Asians work harder. They simply work smarter. Their politicians look upon them as partners, not as criminals.

4. Check out the curriculum being taught in your local schools and see if it is anti-free-market biased. It would shock most Americans to realize that a great deal of the economic information being fed their children in grammar schools, high schools, and especially state universities is blatantly socialistic, if not openly communistic.

The only place that communism seems to still flourish is in the American classroom. It is often labeled "socialism" but, in reality, it is the same doctrine that was taught in Russia prior to the Communist collapse: Government is the protector of the downtrodden; capitalism is inherently evil; everyone deserves a decent income regardless of his desire to work or not; and last, the government is a better purveyor of the nation's resources than are the wage earners.

If you don't believe this is what is being taught to your children, write and ask for a copy of the National Education Association's annual agenda. Or better yet, just check out a copy of your child's civics book and read it.

5. Last, and most important, we as Christians must return to our foundation: Jesus Christ. It is clear that we are not battling against flesh and blood but against principalities and powers. How else can anyone explain what is happening? Rational, intelligent people are destroying the very system that has yielded so much for all of us, and yet they don't see it.

A dear friend of mine once said about Christianity, "If it doesn't work for you, please don't export it." I agree with that sentiment totally. If we can't get our own finances under control and learn to live on what we make, how can we demand that the government do so?

If we continue to take handouts from the government, how can we speak out against government waste? To take a stand against waste means that God's people must also refuse to take FHA or VA loans. Christian farmers need to say, "Thanks, but no thanks, Uncle." Churches need to take care of their own poor, rather than expecting welfare or Medicare to do so.

In short, it means "walking our talk." James said in his letter: "But prove yourselves doers of the word, and not merely hearers who delude themselves" (James 1:22).

I believe I have done what the Lord asked of me: I have warned you. If I am wrong and you do all the things I have suggested, the worst that can happen is that you will end up out of debt and be more involved with our political system.

If I am right and you do nothing, you'll end up losing everything you own and be totally dependent on the very system that created the mess we are facing. Keep in mind that God has everything under control. You can do your part by giving sacrificially to the Lord's work; if you do, you cannot lose. "Because of the proof given by this ministry they will glorify God for your obedience to your confession of the gospel of Christ, and for the liberality of your contribution to them and to all" (2 Corinthians 9:13).

Just as the day of the Lord will come as a thief in the night, so an economic collapse will come in the midst of what appears to be economic prosperity. The very debt that creates the prosperity ultimately destroys it.

If you truly surrender your finances to God, you will experience His faithfulness. I pray the Lord will give you the wisdom to do as He directs you.

In His love,

LARRY BURKETT

Appendix A

The Problem of Government Waste

1. The following is reprinted with permission of Macmillan Publishing Company from *Burning Money: The Waste of Your Tax Dollars,* by J. Peter Grace. Copyright ©1984 by The Foundation for the President's Private Sector Survey on Cost Control, Inc. Mr. Grace served as chairman of President Reagan's Private Sector Survey on Cost Control (the Grace Commission).

The Federal government is the world's largest: power producer, insurer, lender, borrower, hospital system operator, landowner, tenant, holder of grazing land, timber seller, grain owner, warehouse operator, ship owner, and truck fleet operator. The Federal government owns and operates 436,000 non-military vehicles. It has over 17,000 computers, 332 accounting systems, and over 100 payroll systems.

However, while many of the functions performed by business and government are comparable, there is an important difference. Business has to perform those functions efficiently and profitably if it is to survive. That is the discipline of the marketplace and competition ensures that an individual company simply cannot afford to maintain a bloated payroll or mismanage its cash or pay more than it has to for the goods and services it purchases. . . .

American taxpayers, however, allow their government to escape the discipline of the marketplace. We have given government a free hand to mismanage our affairs. We have done this by voting for Congressmen and Senators who have no conception of the terrible consequences that deficit spending will bring.

Managing Money. The [U.S.] government handles some $6.8 billion in transactions a day . . . but despite these enormous sums the government is years behind the private sector in developing modern budgeting and accounting systems. Nor is it familiar with the common business techniques of cash, loan, and debt management. Each department uses its own accounting systems (there are 332 incompatible accounting systems), making accurate government-wide analysis impossible. The government has issued, backed, or sponsored $848 billion in loans outstanding, but lacks adequate controls and thus is highly vulnerable to substantial losses due to error or outright fraud. Government budgeting is mainly concerned with getting next year's spending levels approved, while, in the private sector, results versus what was budgeted in previous years are also examined. Compared to private business, Federal budgeting is done in a vacuum, where past budgets are forever forgotten, and there is little accountability. The Federal government has an annual cash flow of $1.7 trillion; however, cash-management procedures are so poor that money sits idle in non-interest-bearing accounts, costing taxpayers billions of dollars each year.

Will the Real Budget Please Stand Up? The Federal budget greatly understates the true level of Federal activity. First, the government practice of "offsetting" (deducting from spending) amounts collected from loan repayments and the like distorts the picture of actual spending levels. Then, the "off-budget" Federal Financing Bank hides more government spending by offering the Federal agencies a "back door" to the Treasury. . . .

The Impact of Not Buying Prudently. In fiscal 1982, a typical year, the Federal government bought $159 billion in goods and services. Sixty billion dollars of that went for military weapons, the remainder for various goods and services across government. Some $41 billion worth of inventories were stored in hundreds of locations around the country. But the 130,000 Federal procurement personnel—government shoppers—find it difficult to recognize a bargain when they see one. First, they are entangled in over 80,000 pages of procurement regulations, plus 20,000 pages of revisions each year. Besides that, they work with inaccurate information, and their buying is often poorly planned and uncoordinated. You've read stories of the government paying $91 for a 3-cent hardware store screw. What is even more worrisome is that the big items—aircraft, turbines, rockets—are not bought with any greater concern for how much is paid out. The opportunity for fraud and abuse is immense. It is shameful but true that some government contractors get rich by hugely overcharging the government. . . .

The Cost of Not Watching the Store. The Federal government doesn't pay enough attention to the little things—housekeeping, travel, freight, mailing, printing, and so on; it doesn't even know how much many of these functions cost in total. They never tote this up and never look back. The result is excessive costs amounting to tens of billions of dollars a year. But there's no incentive to watch these activities. In fiscal 1982, the government spent $4.8 billion on employee travel. Because of the amount of travel, the government ought to have an in-house travel service, as most corporations do, to negotiate discounts and to efficiently book employee travel. But again, nobody in Washington cares about details. It isn't their money that they're wasting—it's yours. . . .

At the start of our commission's work, we were appalled at the Federal government's lack of basic information on its own activities. Some records aren't kept for more than a year, and others are not kept at all. Some figures are available for certain years but not others. . . .

When we started our work, we tried to find out how many social programs there are. "Oh, about one hundred and twenty-five," we were told. Then we found the book *Fat City*, which describes hundreds of Federal programs that give money away for nonessential purposes—at the expense of taxpayers. We went back to the drawing board and spent six months looking into the question of how many government social programs there are. We found that there are 963 social programs. Somebody in Washington should have known the correct answer—125 was only 13 percent of the true total. That's what we found out over and over again in Washington—somebody should know, but nobody does. . . .

2. Some recent examples of what your taxes are paying for (sources: Citizens Against Government Waste, the Heritage Foundation, and the National Taxpayers Union):

- $49 million for a rock-and-roll museum
- $15 million to Dartmouth College as part of a jobs-creation program—a total of thirty-nine jobs were created, at a cost of $324,685 each
- $1.36 million for preliminary work on an $18.6 million project to turn Miami Boulevard into an "exotic garden for people"
- $566 million (rising to $900 million later in 1991) to send American cows to Europe to participate in an "Export Enhancement Program"
- $500,000 to study the effects of cigarette smoking on dogs
- $107,000 to study the mating habits of Japanese quail
- $19 million to study whether belching by cows and other livestock harms the ozone
- $84,000 to study why people fall in love
- $50,000 to prove that sheepdogs do, in fact, protect sheep
- $46,000 to determine how long it takes to cook breakfast eggs

- **$90,000** to study the social and behavioral aspects of vegetarianism

- **$219,592** to teach college students how to watch television

- **$2,500** to investigate the causes of rudeness, lying, and cheating on tennis courts

- **$25,000** to find the best location for a new gym for the House of Representatives

- **$2 million** to renovate one of the House restaurants

- **$350,000** to renovate the House beauty parlor

- **$6 million** to upgrade the Senate subway system

3. Organizations working to fight government waste and inefficiency:

   Americans to Limit Congressional Terms
   900 2d Street N.E., Suite 200
   Washington, D.C. 20002

   > Donation includes a subscription to their newsletter

   Citizens Against Government Waste
   1301 Connecticut Avenue N.W., Suite 400
   Washington, D.C. 20036

   > Donation includes a subscription to the newsletter "Government Wastewatch"

   Citizens for a Sound Economy
   470 L'enfant Plaza S.W.
   East Building, Suite 7112
   Washington, D.C. 20024

   > Membership is $15 and includes a subscription to the newsletter "On Alert"

Freedom Alliance
P.O. Box 96700
Washington, D.C. 20090

> Donation includes a subscription to the newsletter "The Free American"

National Taxpayer's Union
325 Pennsylvania Avenue S.E.
Washington, D.C. 20003

> Membership is $15, including a subscription to the newsletter "Dollars & Sense"

Appendix B
Resource Material

I. Articles and Excerpts
  A. Information provided by the Federal Reserve.
    1. Federal receipts, outlays, and debt, 1981-92.
    2. Government employment and finances, 1791-1970.
    3. Public debt of the federal government, 1791-1970.
    4. Federal budget summary 1945-1989.
  B. World Facts in Brief. Chicago: Rand McNally & Co., 1986.
  C. Administrative Office of the U.S. Courts Annual Reports, 1988.
  D. Health, a Concern for Every American. Wylie, Tex.: Information Plus, 1991.
    Energy, An Issue of the 90s. Wylie, Tex.: Information Plus, 1991.
  E. U.S. Bureau of Census, 1988, 1990.
  F. Facts on File World News Digest. New York: Facts on File, Dec. 1985, Dec. 1989, Dec. 1990.
  G. Economic Indicators. Washington, D.C.: U.S. Government Printing Office, May 1991.

H. Robert Pollin. Deeper in Debt. Washington, D.C.: Economic Policy Institute, Nov. 1990.

I. A Survey of Current Business. U.S. Bureau of Economic Analysis, June 1989.

II. Book and Pamplet References

A. *War on Waste*. The President's Private Sector Survey on Cost Control. New York: Macmillan, 1984.

B. Harry E. Figgie, Jr. *Tackle the Debt Before It's Too Late*. Figgie International Public Affairs Department, 4420 Sherwin Road, Willoughby, OH 44094.

C. Bruce Wetterau. *The New York Public Library Book of Chronologies*. New York: Prentice-Hall, 1990.

D. Ravi Batra. *The Great Depression of 1990*. New York: Simon & Schuster, 1987.

E. *The McGraw-Hill Dictionary of Modern Economics*. New York: McGraw-Hill, 1973.

F. Gerald Swanson. *The Hyperinflation Survival Guide*. Willoughby, OH: Figgie International, 1989.

G. James McKeever. *End Times Digest*. Omega Ministries, Box 0, Eagle Point, OR.

H. Arthur Zeikel. *History as a Guide*. Merrill Lynch Asset Management, 1991.

I. Ludwig Von Mises. "Money, Method, and the Marketplace" (essays). Norwell, MA: Kluwer Academic Publishers, 1990.

J. James Joy Ferris. *Inflation: The Ultimate Graven Image*. Harrison, AR: New Leaf, 1982.

K. James McKeever. *The AIDS Plague*. Medford, OR: Omega Publications, 1986.